P.O.E.T.®

Anthology

VOLUME VI

inner child press, ltd.

P.O.E.T. PUBLISHING

"Don't allow success or your talents go to your head and cause you to develop a mentality that you are superior to everyone around you. Even in success, you need to have a grateful and thankful heart."

General Information

P.O.E.T. Anthology

People Of Extraordinary Talent
Volume VI

1st Edition : 2019

This Publishing is protected under Copyright Law as a "Collection". All rights for all submissions are retained by the Individual Author and or Artist. No part of this Publishing may be Reproduced, Transferred in any manner without the prior **WRITTEN CONSENT** of the "Material Owner" or its Representative Inner Child Press. Any such violation infringes upon the Creative and Intellectual Property of the Owner pursuant to International and Federal Copyright Law. Any queries pertaining to this "Collection" should be addressed to Publisher of Record.

Publisher Information
1st Edition : Inner Child Press :
intouch@innerchildpress.com
www.innerchildpress.com

This Collection is protected under U.S. and International Copyright Laws

Copyright © 2019 : People Of Extraordinary Talent

ISBN-13 : 978-1-970020-95-3 (inner child press, ltd.)

$ 24.95

Cover Design : Jay Covers

Dedication

This Offering is Dedicated to

P.O.E.T.®

and the Gifts of their Spirit

they give back to the Community of Humanity

through their Spoken Words and Ministries.

"Anything worth having is worth
the trouble and sacrifice to get it."

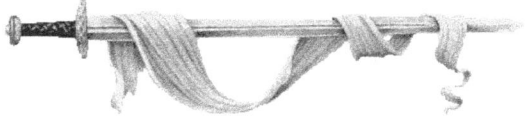

Table of Contents

a few words from Blaq Ice	*i*
a few words from Toy McCray	*xi*
a few words from Lovely Lyricist	*xiii*
a few words from Tony Briscoe	*xv*

THE POETS

Blaq Ice	1
Word Warrior	15
Ameeda Mawalin	27
Dubceez	37
Terri L. Johnson	47
Monica Gray	57
Lady Jo	65
The Endurer	73
Mz. Nina	85
Brazen	93
Poetic Rain	107

Table of Contents ... *continued*

Lady Di	115
Lovely Lyricist	121
Dr. H.	135
William S. Peters, Sr.	143

EPILOGUE 157

P.O.E.T. FALLEN SOLDIERS 159

P.O.E.T. PICTURES 167

P.O.E.T. WEB LINKS 187

P.O.E.T.'S OTHER ANTHOLOGIES 189

a few words from Blaq Ice

Out of every generation there comes a movement produced out of the frustration of the people in a longing for change. P.O.E.T. People Of Extraordinary Talent is the movement that has brought forth that change to the Spoken Word community in America. They have literally changed their words into actions. From mentoring in schools, to giving away scholarships to disadvantaged children, to visiting homeless shelters and prisons, P.O.E.T has revolutionized the game. P.O.E.T has been on the move and is a vanguard in the artist activist community. This book is the 6th volume of the P.O.E.T anthology series and contain words of wisdom, inspiration and motivation. We pray that this book blesses you and that you find something in it that you can share with others. We are truly honored by your support and we promise we will continue to Change The World, One Heart, One Mind, One Verse At A Time.

Blaq Ice aka De'Andre Hawthorne

P.O.E.T. (People of Extraordinary Talent)
International President & Founder
CEO & Founder of the National Spoken Word AWARDS

Email: kingofspokenwordblaqice@gmail.com
Website: www.blaqice.com
Math: 312.719.7310

a few words from *Toy McCray Hawthorne*

I am extremely proud of our 6th anthology book. As titled, this is truly a BREAKTHROUGH moment in our organization. The P.O.E.T movement has weathered the storm of members who have come and gone, members who have passed away, yet we keep growing and going strong. This year has been one of our most successful and productive years. This has been our BREAKTHROUGH year. We have embraced the challenges and come out shining on the other side. We have monthly mentorship programs at Cook Elementary school and the Impact Family Center. We have a bi-monthly program at the Cook County Juvenile Detention Center. Our members have stepped out on their own, with our support, creating their own mentorship and community programs and are making a difference. As Vice President of this organization I look forward to this book release, celebrating our members and watching them achieve their goals. Lastly, if you are struggling to do some of the things we are already achieving, we are still open for membership.

Toy Ann McCray Hawthorne
Blaq Isis

International Vice President
P.O.E.T®
People of Extraordinary Talent
toyannmccray@yahoo.com

a few words from *Lovely Lyricist*

As we embark on The P.O.E.T® Anthology 6th edition, *Breakthrough*, I can't help but to go back to volume one and think on how we began and how nervous we all were becoming a published author. I can still feel the excitement of when the first volume was in the possession of our President Blaq Ice! I watched the video and screamed because he opened it and was showing my name, picture and work in print. I was totally excited not simply because I had become a published author yet more because this meant people all over the world can share in the experience of my gift of our gifts.

The artist and poets sharing in this volume, just as others, have managed to give in many ways while still living this thing called life! Their struggles, pain, sweat and tears did not prevent them from sharing the gifts afforded to them by God and my prayer is simply that everyone who has the ability to experience the words on these pages are able to know that they are shared with the mindset to help heal the hearts, minds and spirits of those in need of healing yet to also being smiles the faces of those in need of laughter and joy.

I thank all who shared and all who will read ~ Lovely

Sincerely,

Antoinette 'Lovely Lyricist' Coleman

International Chairperson
P.O.E.T. (People of Extraordinary Talent)

lovelysoulfulessentials@gmail.com

a few words from *Tony Briscoe*

The P.O.E.T® Anthology Series expands to its 6th edition. Forever etched in stone, this Breakthrough volume cuts to the core of a team that has weathered tumult, change, death, opposition, and conflict, all while remaining one of the most impactful community arts organizations in Chicago.

From our own pockets we donate, travel, support, uplift, and give back to society. Be it in Indiana, Michigan, Wisconsin, Africa, Jamaica, or Indonesia, the P.O.E.T organization expands the globe. No matter what we endure you can rest assured we will always BREAKTHROUGH.

Sincerely,

Tony Briscoe aka The Endurer

Advisory Board President
P.O.E.T. (People of Extraordinary Talent)

endurer@gmail.com

"Every one of us up in here
faces some type of challenge daily.
It's up to you to find a way to overcome it."

P.O.E.T.®

Official Seal

If you don't give up on you, He won't ! Always remember family you're number one.

~Michael "Big Mike" Anthony

P.O.E.T.

Anthology

VOLUME VI

inner child press, ltd.

P.O.E.T. PUBLISHING

Tradition has Gotten us where we are,
Change will carry us into the future.

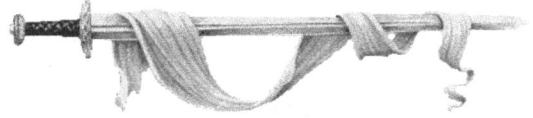

P.O.E.T. ANTHOLOGY VOLUME VI

BLAQ ICE

De'Andre Hawthorne

BLAQ ICE AKA DE'ANDRE HAWTHORNE

P.O.E.T. ANTHOLOGY VOLUME VI

KING OF POETRY BLAQ ICE

Once in a lifetime, society is blessed with a rare spirit that brings forth cultural change, sets new standards of greatness and serves as a sacrifice for future generations. BLAQ ICE IS ONE OF THE GREATEST SPOKEN WORD ENTERTAINERS OF HIS GENERATION.

Blaq Ice is an Award Winning, American poet, International Spoken Word life artist, entertainer, lecturer, promoter, producer, host, published author, mentor and activist, with over 30 year in the game. The contributions of this amazing artist to American and Chicago spoken word poetry is truly Monumental. Blaq Ice made history by establishing the 1st National Spoken Word Awards in 2017.

In 2019, Blaq Ice won his 6th Chicago Music award, his 5th for best poet. He produced and released 3 albums, totaling 26 album releases so far. He toured internationally and taught his poetry at East-West University college.

Not only has he left an imprint in the Spoken Word Genre internationally, but he has also left his footprint in communities across America with his artist/activist movement P.O.E.T, inspiring thousands of ordinary people to use their gifts to do extraordinary works in their communities.

www.blaqice.com
twitter: BlaqIcePoetKing
Instagram: kingofpoetryblaqice
kingofspokenwordblaqice@gmail.com

BLAQ ICE AKA DE'ANDRE HAWTHORNE

STAY HUMBLE

There's a lot of things in life
That we take 4 granted
And 2 be quite candid
When somebody takes advantage
Of your love I can't stand it

I know some of y'all who take your man
Through the ringer
Bleeding him dry
While U brag every day about
Having that man wrapped around your finger

What goes around comes around
And a man is at his most vulnerable
When he let his guard down
Oh, U wanna act funny now

I remember when I 1st met U
U stayed with your Momma
In a house full of people
Living in everyday drama

Well I know a chick named Karma
Have U seen her
She comes around every once in a while
I really don't think U want 2 meet her

STAY HUMBLE

They say that shivery is dead
But U took it 2 another level
Made sure she never had 2 settle
And eventually moved her 2 the burbs
From the ghetto

Building a future, making everything tight
Like Luther, If only 4 one night
Got her right where U wanted her

Then U got all big headed
Headed down the wrong path
And now she dreads it
U Went from a premium dude 2 unleaded

Yeah, I said it
Now U can't even answer her phone calls
U don't even wanna come home at all
It's more important 2 hang out
With your boys and play ball

Life is cold, but it's fair
One day your ass came home
2 an empty house
And no one was there

STAY HUMBLE

The moral of the story is
When U do right, right will follow U
When U do wrong, wrong will catch U

And I bet some of U wish
U could go back and do things differently
Treat your relationships more gently
Because Hindsight is 20/20

And never treat the one U with
Like the one U had
Cause once a good girl's gone bad
She's gone forever

And it takes a man a long time 2 feel
Once his heart has been killed
He'll dog every woman thereafter
Until his heart is healed

Be real and 2 thine own self be true
Treat your significant other
Like U would want them 2 treat U
STAY HUMBLE

BEHIND CLOSED DOORS

Common threads make for strange bed fellows
Normally when 2 walk together, 1 is in the shadows
These voice tones be sonic like Seattle
Smooth, yet, I battle with betrayal

It never fails, with some of these males who act like females
When times get rough, they bail
Switching lanes, while I blaze trails
On a scale from 1 to 10, they all fail

Or fall off
2 soft 4 struggle
And 2 lazy 4 the hustle

They figure it's easier to be at ease
But can't see the forest 4 the trees
U not succeeding was never on me
It seemed I was hard on U
Because I could see in U more than U could see

Weak minds speak lies of blasphemy
I'm not saying I'm almighty
But I created a fire in U more than
U had ever seen

You'd do anything 2 be seen
even abandon your team
Kissing asses and rings
on the other side the grass and always green

I can see the evil in your eyes
Snakes always come in disguise
I just keep on looking for the signs
I'm just a south side brother from the chi

Living this life on the fly
I just sit here sometimes and wonder why

U better keep them eyes on the prize
Lord I just wanna testify

Success tastes so sweet
No matter who's feet U step on
No matter who's back U get on

U didn't arrive here all by your lonely
But now U want to phony kick it
Like you've punched your own ticket
I don't get it

Always give credit where credit is due
U act like U forgot who mentored U
And when U come around mediocrity abounds in U
Hypocrisy found in U
All U can say is what U meant 2 do
Yet, I still forgive U
There's an old saying, don't bite the hand that feeds U

I knew U were a devil, but I still chose U
U only did what U were supposed 2
I prayed 4 a blessing and it came in U

Lord remove anyone from me that has ill will in their heart
And he used U, U helped make that prayer come true
Everyone U poised left with U

It made us stronger
Now, we no longer deal with jealousy and envy
I swear 2 God frienemies are worse than enemies

BLAQ ICE AKA DE'ANDRE HAWTHORNE

STEAL IT

It's something about the lust of a man
Who puts his hunger in his hands
And expands a plan to take what he can
Out of something he can't have from that one woman

He's feeling it so much
That even the slightest touch arouses him
Affects him, erects him
More like special effects he hallucinates

She's stays on his mind constantly
He goes 2 sleep and wakes with the same thought
Caught up due 2 no fault of his own
Strong-armed by denial

Every crocked half smile and dimple
Which seems so simple, cripples him
Sending ripple effects down his spine
He tries 2 conceal it, he can't help but 2 feel it
Damn it, he has 2 STEAL IT

She's exactly what he's been waiting 4
The more he sees her, the more he wants her
Cards and flowers, he confronts her
And would never do anything 2 disappoint her

She minds her own business
Infatuated, her mind becomes his business
She's wrapped in thickness
Like a gift 4 Christmas, although he doesn't celebrate

Let Jehovah be his witness
He's knocking on doors that ain't opened
Hoping 4 that one opportunity
These thoughts be guilty as sin
Lord have mercy, grant him immunity

She's the itch that he can't seem 2 scratch
The catch that caused him 2 finally meet his match
Already attached, he can't seem 2 hold back
He gotta STEAL IT

This is the moment that he's been waiting for
He adores her and it oozes from his pores
Never before has a woman shook him at his core
Like this one

A match made in heaven
He's an artist and she's a beautiful work of art
He's not trying 2 steal 2 fulfill his sexual desires
The only thing on his mind is stealing her heart

FLY THE W

Let's go 2 work
It's A new season
And a new reason 2 cheer
Once it's again it's that time of the year
Baseball season is here

And I'm riding with the North side
Chi-Town
Windy City
My Town

And we hungry this year
Central Division champs, 1st place
Stakes are high
Batter up, we are looking for the home plate

And it's no better time
Than the friendly confines
In the summer time
So let us rewind to 2016

It's no longer a dream
We'll get there some way some how
We ain't waiting til next year
We want it right now

So everybody put those W's up
And let me feel U
In the words of Harry Carry
A 1, a 2, a 3, Let me hear U

FLY THE W

A championship journey
Starts with one step
And we ain't gone stop
Until we are the only ones left standing

Number 1 in the standings
We got the best players on the field
And the best 10th man and
The best 10th man?
Yeah, the best fans

And every victory will be in the memory
Of all the Cubs Greats
From Santos to Sandberg to William's
To Mr. Cub Ernie Banks

Maddox, Dawson and Grace
Bruce Sutter, Fergie Jenkins
Hack Wilson
And Gabby 4 his 19 years behind the plate

So let's kick it with the Rickets
Start preparing now 4 your
World Series tickets

And tuning in day by day
Play by play
Harry carry tell em
what you've U have 2 say
Hey Hey Hey

THE LAST STRAW

Over 19 years ago
We came into each other lives
U birthed something inside of me
That I thought had died

A long time ago
That night U inspired me 2 write
Started a career that would last my whole life
Without U, there never would have been a Blaq Ice

We traveled the world
Hit some of the biggest stages
Sometimes we would argue fuss and fight
U know how relationships go through phases

It's funny how we always assume
That the ones whom we love will always be in the room close enough 2 touch
But never in a million years
Did I ever think I would be losing U this soon

THE LAST STRAW

I don't know what I'm supposed 2 feel right now
But whatever it is, I'm feeling it
All I know is one thing
God's will can't be this

This feeling is all to familiar
Butterflies in stomach
Frog in throat
Emotionally overwhelmed, trying 2 cope
With the news of losing U
2 a terminal illness, no antidote

One of the strongest people I know
You've had 2 fight your whole life

Little did the world know
You were in a fight 4 your life

Don't wanna talk 2 nobody or see nobody
What am I supposed 2 do?
I can't imagine what this poetry world
Will be without U

I doubt U really knew how much U were loved
And appreciated
Years from now it will be debated

Arguably U will go down as the undisputed
Queen of Erotic Poetry
Period, end of STORY

I'm glad that we rocked out together
We loss U the last day of Winter
I guess that winters be the coldest weather
I will never ever forget U, I will love U forever
I guess this is the last straw

I got the call on Tuesday March 19
Somewhere around 4
E said, Ice man I think U better get over here
15 minutes later I was knocking on the door

Damn, I was too late
This is way too much
After I embraced Candace and John
I kissed your forehead
U were still warm 2 the touch

Family and friends begin 2 gather at the house
Reminiscing about the good times
Some laughs some cries
I prayed in the spirit while I wrote this piece on the couch

BLAQ ICE AKA DE'ANDRE HAWTHORNE

I was hoping U were going 2 get better
We were supposed 2 take over Vegas together
Never can anyone say U didn't share your stage
Through U, there were a lot of careers made

A lot of people paid
There was a method 2 the madness
Verbal Intercourse spiced up many marriages
And a lot of relationships were saved
And if U had 2 do it all over again
I know U wouldn't change a thing

U would do it the same way
U left some big shoes 2 fill
There will never be another who could take your place

It's going 2 take me a minute
2 get myself together
But I promise as long as I live
Your Legacy will live on 4 ever

I'm going 2 miss my Big Sis & friend
And until we meet again
I'll hold on 2 God's word, Revelations 21:4
We may have loss the battle
But I promise U, we'll win the war

THE LAST STRAW

P.O.E.T. ANTHOLOGY VOLUME VI

WORD WARRIOR

Edward Felton

WORD WARRIOR aka EDWARD FELTON

WORD WARRIOR aka EDWARD FELTON

Every so often, one comes along and changes the course history, as it had once been known. This unique artist has changed the perception of a Spoken Word artist, blending his own brand of spirituality, pesonal testimony and an articulated style of pronounced words to the game. When Chicago writes down it's history on Spoken Word, I have no doubt that the name WORD WARRIOR is worthy to be mentioned amongst those who have had a major impact in the Spoken Word genere.

WORD WARRIOR aka Eddie B was born Edward "Eddie" Felton, in the Auburn-Gresham neighborhood on Chicago's south side. He attended Mayfair Dance Academy elementary school where he took modern dance classes and excelled in his on unique creative style of dance, winning multiple talent showcases, making him a natural on stage. The feeling of winning was so amazing for Eddie that, for the first time, he saw how working hard would pay off. His dance instructor was so impressed that he performed his own choreographed routine, combining street and classical modern dance. He would take his routine from the school to the community block club parties and was well received by his neighbors and friends. While in elementary school something significant would take place that would affect Eddie's future a great deal. He saw a bike that he really wanted, however, his father refused to purchase it for him unless he memorized a poem called SUCCESS written in a book entitled THINK AND GROW RICH by Napoleon Hill. This would be the spark that would ignite a fire inside of his spirit to become interested in reading and ultimately writing poetry.

Today Word Warrior is an award winning Poet, Spoken Word Artist, Radio Talk Show Host, Public Speaker and Mentor.

Contact Info :

Telephone : 773.354.3582
Email : wordwarrior73@gmail.com

QUEEN

You are the "Mother" Of this Earth
You are royalty
Know your worth
You are a "Goddess" to your man
You are a princess throughout the land
You are the right hand to the throne
Stand firm my sister Claim your own
You are the voice
Of the community
Be proud
My sisters
And stand in unity
You come in so many shades it
And so many colors
And such an asset
TO the King and Bro
Where Will the world be Without your presence? so much loveliness And so much essence
You have stood tall
Through so many generations
You are such an upliftment
TO the nation
You are the backbone Of the family
Without You Queen
Where would we be?
Grandmother
M 0th er Sisters so true
Without You Queens
We wouldn't have made it through
I salute you Queen
You have withstood your stance
You have shown you're able
Without your man
TO all my Queens
I dedicate this to you
Just keep on doing
What you do

What Happens In The Black Family

I was just Sitting and wondering
What was the origin
Of Why the Black family splits
Before it begins
I mean
I'm just trying to figure out
Why we can it keep
Unity inside our own house
The sister has the Child
Everything is COOl for a while
Before you know it
There's arguing, bickering, commotions repeated All Of a sudden
The Black family has been deleted
I don't want to paint the finger
At the woman or the man
But deep down
Truly and mentally
I don't understand
Why is our percentage Of break up so high
Why are we permanently labeled
Baby mama
Baby daddy
I don't know Why
I mean some relationships work
Some marriages do too
But the majority Of broken homes
IS through the roof
I really want to know
What is the basis Of this course
I mean
Why can't the black relationships work
I really think it'S sad
There's always a mom at home
But no dad
What is the solution to this scenario
Can it be turned around
IS it possible

WORD WARRIOR aka EDWARD FELTON

Single parent homes
Why does this begin
Mom is raising the children by herself
When does that end
Break-ups
Fallout
Di votes
Split—ups
Why can't we change
The nature Of this negative Stuff
What happens in the Black family
Can someone please help me out Can we turn negatives into positives so we can have a better foundation in our own house

The Struggle Is Real

Do you know What it is to have
Then have not?
Do you know how it feels to be ballin' then be popped!
Struggle is interesting
It teaches you humbleness
Confidence
Concentration and Organization so many issues
Trying to make it to your goal so many hurdles Will make you explode!
You have to reach down inside
Because you want to get it right
You have to reach way down inside and just FIGHT!
FIGHT!
FIGHT!
The struggle is very real and I tell you no lie
The struggle is very real and
I don't know Why
The struggle is real
I guess it makes you and
Molds you
Once you overcome the struggle
It does not control you
Bumps and bruises
You and endured along the way
Experience and lessons
Make you Who you are today
It's like climbing a hill and
Once you make it to the top
Success and positive mindset
Just Will not Stop
You got in the race
Thinking you're going to Win
You got in the race
With all hands in
You 've endured the race and Some things just didn't work
You didn't Win the race
NOW your feelings are hurt

WORD WARRIOR aka EDWARD FELTON

I guess without struggle It wouldn't be life
I guess without struggle
It wouldn't be right
Struggle teaches you patience
Struggle teaches you appreciation Struggle teaches you respect so you can comprehend
life'S tests Struggle is a journey and
I'm thankful for this lesson
Struggle can be rough and
I'm thankful for the blessing
In closing...
I don't know how you feel
But I must tell you
That the struggle is real

In Love With Poetry

AS I embrace you on internet radio shows
And embrace you on the Stage
AS I grab the mic and hold it firmly
It's you that I engage
You are my therapy
You Are My Breath
You Are My craving
From now on until my death
If I could marry you
I would do it in a heartbeat
I even recite you
In my deepest Sleep
What did you really do to me Because
I'm poetry crazy!
AS you can see
You grabbed my heart and
Turned it inside out
You run through my mind
Leaving footprints
Without a doubt
I'm love With you
And there's no cure
Only words
And metaphors And expression
I can endure
My passion and craving
Cannot be matched
I'm in so deep
I can't turn back I'm in love With you
You are my oxygen
I never ever want my life to end
I am you
You are me
Poetry has reformed SOMETHING
If you were the only woman
Left in this world

WORD WARRIOR aka EDWARD FELTON

We would die together
AS you are my girl
I love you more than life itself
I love you
More than my health,
I love you
With everything I have
I love you so much
I need rehab

Two Praying Grandmothers

I had two praying grandmother's, They both prayed real hard, Without those praying grandmothers, I wouldn't have made it this far,
Coming up as a Child I was always blessed
Stayed in church
In Sunday's best
TWO sets Of grandparents
That's spoiled me on both ends
TOYS and Gifts
Until there was no end Birthdays and Christmas
Were always superb and
My two praying grandmothers
Made sure I always received the word
It was so much fun
Switching grandparents house
Every other weekend
I Wish I could relive that Stage
All over again
I had two praying grandmother's, They both prayed real hard, Without those praying grandmothers. I wouldn't have made it this far,
I went through my stages Of adolescence
With a few scrapes and bruises It was nothing but the blessings
I wasn't an angel
I did my share
But now I realized
Those prayers were there Even through High School
I was a hot mess
Between gangbanging and girls
I kept my family stressed
Through prayers and discipline I graduated on time
I thank those praying grandmother's Of mine
I lost a lot Of friends to bullets
That didn't pull through
It was my two praying grandmother's I thought you knew!
I had two praying grandmother's, They both prayed real hard, Without those praying grandmothers. I wouldn't have made it this far,

so humble and thankful For those two strong women
That sent up prayers and
All the favor I was given
Every other weekend I stayed in church so I truly know that prayer really works so you may ask me
HOW do you survive for years in Chicago
It was the prayers Of my grandmothers
I want you to know
Rest in peace
TO my grandmothers
They have moved on
You better believe those prayers
Still remain strong

P.O.E.T. ANTHOLOGY VOLUME VI

AMEEDAH MAWALIN

AMEEDAH MAWALIN

AMEEDAH MAWALIN

Ameedah Mawalin (Author Ramona Sapphire-Bodi) was born and raised in Chicago's Hyde Park community. She enjoys writing short stories and novels on assorted topics based on experience and overall—imagination, and that are relatable able. She admits she's a bit eccentric and quirky.

Additionally, Ameedah has been a spoken word artist and performer since 1996 and dishes out a mean cup of coffee to her audiences upon popular demand. This signature piece is entitled, Midnight Brew. She has written, performed, and sold several volumes of poetry, business booklets, and stories beginning in the early nineties.

Ameedah has been recently published and is also the self-publisher of other works. In 2019 Ameedah joined the international P.O.E.T (People Of Extraordinary Talent) organization and began to tour her work. With P.O.E.T She has made appearances at the Bantu Fest, the African Fest, the National Spoken Word Awards and the Soulful Book Fair. She received a Firekeeper Award at the 2019 P.O.E.T awards and this is just the first of many awards to come.

Ameedah can be found on Twitter, Tumblr, Facebook, and reached at her website at www.sapphirewithpassion.com. Texting: 773-981-7409

AMEEDAH MAWALIN

SPENT

She was simply incredible. Now don't get me wrong, I don't flow like that. It's just that she was beyond awesome. She had me spent, alright. I became her stalker. I followed her everywhere that day, to work, the grocer, and home. I ogled her from afar, timing her comings and goings like clockwork. I scanned her from head to toe and admired every inch of her. She was a splendiferous road map of extraordinary bumps and curves. She wasn't flawless by any means, but I could get past that. After all, no one could claim perfection. Even if her exterior was perfect, there's no telling what lurked interiorly.

I began with her fabulous forehead, magnificently shaped, with a drizzle of fuzz around her temples. Next, I headed toward her bridge but began with the forest preceding it. She had a mane richer and more sparkly than coal, and brows perfectly-shaped to-live-for. I now crossed the bridge down the wide path. Previous to that, I'd gazed into her globes, clear as a fresh-water creek. Her enchanting windows projected her soul, transparent as unstained glass. Presently at the bridge, I made it over to her razzle-dazzle blood-red-painted lips that were full and juicy. She puckered them teasingly, perhaps beckoning a succulent sultry kiss. My probing eyes hungrily slid down the sensuous slope of her neck to her chest, intercepted by two asymmetrical, yet supple perky boulders. These seemingly summoned a long-awaited soothing caress.

I continued down the winding road of her belly and reveled in its core. The road was steep and flawed with scars and protracted, nevertheless magnificent. I longed to massage it, but somehow I was stuck on her imperfections. Then I decided she was okay by me. After all, they represented the legacy of her trials and tribulations and the journey of her being. I rested in her greenery briefly because it was too painful to linger there. It seems there were too many ghosts of pain and shame to count and frankly, I wasn't in that space right now. I was feeling her in a good kinda way. Next, I slid down her sturdy lean poles and landed at her feet. These were scaly and normal-sized with a few ridges and claws. I was appalled, however, judged there was nothing a good manicure couldn't fix. She caught me staring and invited me in. I hesitated at first, then caved in. Next, she allowed me to observe her, and I followed her every move.

She slithered out of her velvety robe and settled in a warm tub of bath salts and lavender rose water. She gently soaked and massaged herself like a newborn. Mellow tones played from piped-in music she'd had installed. The room was quaint with pops of color, divinely-scented flowers, soaps, and candles, with matching bath & shower accessories and luscious rugs and though all this was breathtakingly fabulous, my eyelids would not allow me to proceed much longer. I signaled this to her and she complied. She completed her bath, managed her physical and oral care, and donned her silky pajamas...

I took one last lingering breath and admiring glance at her in the mirror and she smiled back at me. I seized my video camera from the pod and headed to bed. I climbed in and cuddled with her and crashed. I was in love.

Taken from MyLight Zone Book 2, Ramona Sapphire

AMEEDAH MAWALIN

CHANGE FOR a DOLLAH

Mr. Triffle had been financially irresponsible and strapped most of his adult life. Over time, he'd lost relationships, family, and friends.

He'd quit jobs soon after he got them, solely upon the basis that he judged he should be promoted every time he performed minimally well. Due to this rotten attitude, he was unable to sustain any of his financial obligations.

Mr. Triffle had gotten to the point where he'd become homeless. He'd pinned this on all his employers that'd disavowed his worth. Thus he began drinking heavily. He'd dodge detox treatment which caused his isolative derelict homeless lifestyle.

Additionally, Mr. Triffle suffered from severe anxiety and depression and refused treatment for that as well. "Whoa is me," became his mantra. Eventually, he decided to give up and take up the vocation of panhandling rather than taking a look at himself with the possibility of doing better.
Currently, Mr. Triffle is sitting on a stoop watching the pedestrians go by. He accosts a young woman and asks, "Can you spare a dollah?" with a drunken slur.

"No, but I have some change," she responds, sympathetically. "I didn't ask you for no stinkin' change," huffed Mr. Triffle. "I asked you for a dollah!" "Scram!" said the young woman, "Or I'll call the cops if you don't get the hell out of my face!"

Mr. Triffle frightened out of his wits swaggered to another stoop and asked a young man in his drunken slur, "Can you spare a dollah?"

"No. But let me search my pockets and see if I have some change," said the young man, kindly.
"I didn't ask you for no stinkin' change," huffed Mr. Triffle. "I asked you for a dollah!"
"Alrighty then," said the young man. "I'll just be on my way." Mr. Triffle traveled from stoop to stoop and panhandled all over the city and nearby suburbs. He'd ask everyone that passed precisely the identical question in his usual drunken slur, "Can you spare a dollah?" Passerbys would at least offer him change, to which he'd typically responds, "I didn't ask you for no stinkin' change. I asked you for a dollah!"

Mr. Triffle suffered from liver failure due to cirrhosis of the liver and other insurmountable ailments. Tragically, he eventually passed away. People throughout his life had offered advice and guidance, to which he'd refused...
Mr. Triffle could have spared his own life had he'd learned this valuable lesson; that those dollars would never have amounted to anything substantial without change.

EVIDANCE OF BELIEF

We are being watched today by others far and near. They're listening to every word we say and what we truly adhere. God is judging our allegiance by making a humble request, that we all work in unity and be our personal best.

Personal doesn't mean self; it means doing the best you can. It means all for one and one for all, and together we shall stand, from a closed fist to an open hand spreading truth throughout the land.
We've been told within our day where there's a will there's a way. Then if our will is to have our own, some dues we all must pay. Our will should be like iron, an unyielding and stiffened force, that works and pumps and never tires until it fulfills its course.

We're under so much pressure to fight until we have won. Our faith is just a small measure of the work that must be done.

Don't think because you have the truth you're automatically saved. For you'll be judged by what you do and the type of path you've paved.

There are goals that we must reach in order from here we can depart. If you don't practice what you preach, God won't know what's in your heart. Don't permit another's evil and ill to block you from relief. For there are criteria we all must fulfill as evidence of our belief.
Copyright © 1993, Ameedah Mawalin, Ebony Sonnets

BLACK BI-PRODUCTS

1 times the gain = 2 times the pain 1 times the rights = 2 times the fights 1 times dead = 2 times the bloodshed 1 times schooled = 2 times fooled 1 times the abode = 2 times the note 1 times the residence = 2 times the pestilence 1 times the pay = 2 times the outlay 1 times the limit = 2 times trying to spend it 1 time the rut = 2 times stuck 1 times accepted = 2 times rejected 1 times white = 2 times alright 1 times black = 2 times held back 1 times smarter = 2 times harder I times failed = 2 times jailed 1 times hired = 2 times fired 1 times promoted = 2 times devoted 1 times the boss = 2 times the cost 1 times freed = 2 times in need 1 times create = 2 times great 1 times unite = 2 times the might!

MIDNIGHT BREW

You excite my thirst with your mellow aroma. I crave your steamy hot essence at bizarre hours of each day and night. Yet I savor you only by day, for at nightfall you leave me thrashing in wide-eyed frenzy.

When I partake of you, every sip invigorates my taste buds to ecstasy. With every swig of you, I savor your pure black freshness.

I cling to you for energy, enthusiasm, and enlightenment. I binge on you with thirsting passion and devotion. The stroke of you with my lips and tongue turns me out! And without you, I'm groggy, sluggish, devastated---all of which arouses my thirst again. So, I quench my thirst with your rich black substance, again, and again, and again, 'til I've reached my peak.

But, then I crash. The bitterness has swelled in my mouth. Intimidated, you're no longer fresh and responsive to me. Gradually, I've discovered I guzzled too much. Now I'm overwhelmed and delusional and frantic to get you out of.

I Am Poetry . . . . can you hear my song ?

P.O.E.T. ANTHOLOGY VOLUME VI

DUBCEEZ
AKA
THE
AUTHOR

Willie Frank Jones, Jr.

DUBCEEZ ... THE AUTHOR

DUBCEEZ... THE AUTHOR

Dubceez aka The Author, (Willie Frank Jones Jr.) was born December 27,1967 in Chicago, Illinois the eldest of 6 children. Willie grew up on the south side in the Englewood neighborhood.

At a young age during elementary school he gained interest in poetry and started entering poetry contests at Guggenheim elementary school. It was during the 7th grade that Willie started learning and perfecting what today is known as, beat boxing. From the ages 12-19 Willie along with a childhood friend, became one of the most popular local rap groups in Chicago. Battling and defeating some of the best the city had to offer. Willie attended Simeon Vocational High School during the era of the late Ben Wilson and Nick Anderson. Over the years Willie has had the pleasure of performing amongst the likes of Will Smith, Boogie Down Production, Mc Lyte and Eric B and Rakim just to name a few.

In The year 2000 Willie moved to Green Bay where for 16 years, he started and successfully ran his own entertainment company. Dubceez Entertainment which is till this day, responsible for the Dubceez Awards Show as well as the hip hop scene in Green Bay. November 2016 Willie joined P.O.E.T (People Of Extraordinary Talent) where he still at this present time is an active and dedicated member assisting with hosting radio shows and assisting in every way possible.

In 2018, the UNDERGROUND POWER HOUR would go on to win a National Spoken Word Award for best station for Hip Hop and Poetry. In 2019 the Dubceez Awards celebrated it's tenth year anniversary in Chicago. Willie's passion for music and helping others is what keeps him continually striving to make platforms for the next generation.

DUBCEEZ ... THE AUTHOR

WE ARE FAMILY

We are family, I got all my people with me,
We are family, but we all spell it P.O.E.T

Good evening passengers as you are boarding this flight tonight
We hope you are prepared for the celebration... make sure your seat belts are tight

Our destination is locked into the navigation heading to success and it won't change
And we can thank Samuel L Jackson for helping us get all those snakes off the plane

See there's tons of talent in this organization flowing like blood in a vein
Show after show and only one thing has changed

Sometimes the hosts names, egos and pain
Even the most modest leader knew to keep a sharp shooter in range

With a real sharp eye for snakes, fakes and poetic impersonators
So guess who's taken the role as the lethal lyrical hater assassinator

D..U..B..C...E..E...Z
Hired hit-man for the P.O.E.T

But tonight is monumental for the poet radio station oh yeah
It's all kool and the gang cause
There's a party going on right here
A celebration to last throughout the year

So bring yo good time and yo laughter to
We gone celebrate and party with you
Come now

We once again completed a successful event
See it's the obedience and the gift that god has sent

I'd like to thank fans and foes
Amateurs and pros
For making underground power hour their #1 show.

Glad to be part of this successful movement
Best believe that there's still a point to be proven

So as we exit a wonderful and successful night
Family let's start focusing on next year, if you agree let me hear you say...... alright

PAY ATTENTION

I open my eyes in the morning but my body is still asleep
I know there's a soul out there somewhere that really needs me

Be it family or friend or maybe even a stranger
My job is to help... Heal... And remove all danger

I'm not perfect and Jesus Christ I am not
But I have a debt that I owe him one that I've never forgot

If he could've died for me without even knowing I would be born
Then I can reach out and help someone whose life in some form has been torn

Someone may be having a situation with money
Their job or even a place to stay
I'm here to tell you that God has sent me with this message today

He said... Keep your head up, chin out and spirit flying high
If you believe in his powers then by faith you will get by

Sometimes I have to be reminded of what my call in life is
You see it as entertainment but I'm really relaying messages just like this

May you eat from my plate and drink from my glass
Selfishness isn't of a godly form so I leave that to the past

Many people miss out on their blessings due to what we see as pride
Ashamed to ask for help so they continue to be stressed inside

Blessings come in many forms and that's the reason why
I say, be careful of what you overlook so your blessings don't past you by

UNCLE'S LOVE

There are many times In life that we feel pain in our hearts
And when we lose someone.... that's where it always starts

We overlook the good times and we only focus on pain
But when it comes to my uncle Polk
Now that's a different thang

His purpose and goal in life was basically the same
To put a smile on everyone's face so that we could forget the pain

He'd sing, he'd dance and he loved to talk
Somehow he'd end up doing a James Brown split or Michael Jackson moonwalk

No matter what went wrong you could count on Unk to brighten the mood
Cause a party without uncle Polk, was like a Bar B Que with know food

So to my Aunt, Uncle and cousins, I send you all my love
Asking God to comfort you all as a new Angel is signed in above

So Unk, to get past this pain, it might take a while
But just thinking about all the fun we had will help me keep a smile

Love You Uncle Polk

GRANNY

I remember when I first met you I was received with open arms
Fell in love with your cooking and your motherly charm

You'd always hug me and call me your big baby
It was always genuine love, no If ands or maybes

You put trust in me even when I didn't trust myself
You also showed me that it's OK to trust someone else

If I took a seat to write down the names of everyone who's heart you've touched
Then I'd never stand again cause there's so many for whom you've done so much

I'm in disbelief.... it doesn't sound right, my Granny's gone
But the love you instilled in so many people, will carry on
To all the family members, let her love remain in your heart
And continue to display what she was designing from the start

An empire, not of money or material things
But of love for one another and pursuing of dreams

Well Granny, as you make this transition
And sit with our father in the sky
Tell Betty, Diane, Tiffany, Horace, Doug and my dad I said hi.

We all took care of you the best we could
But who can care for you more then he would?
I love you Granny and there was never any doubt,
You showed me what genuine love was all about.

Love DUB.

LETTER 2 MY BROTHER

Today I received a message that I was really in need of hearing
Though I've conquered plenty there was still a little fear in

Inside me was this self-battling rivalry
After 35 years of doing this, the fear still sits inside of me

The preparation and dedication initiates motivation
That's what keeps me soaring like a eagle seeking for migration

Yet the 99% of confidence and know how
Was plagued by that 1% of oh wow
Continues to be the reason Dubceez constantly comes back just when they think I'm down

There are so many people that count on me to be there to prepare the stage
Setting the foundation for many, regardless of race, sex or age

I was listening this morning when Blaq ice was rolling live
You better start catching some of that knowledge on the early morning drive

He was speaking about never letting someone tell you
That you can't reach your dreams
And though he used Lebron metaphorically
I read between the lines and I know just what he mean

Ever since I started the Dubceez awards and events
For every 10 people supporting me I get 20 that think it don't make sense
I sometimes let it get under my skin and taint my mind with doubt
But that message knocked me right back on track and focus on what it's all about

This award show ain't about me although it bares my name
But a sign of obedience to help shape, mold and make stars all the same

Blaq Ice, my brother, it's with the words
That you form pictures in my mind
See we been doing this since way back in time

DUBCEEZ ... THE AUTHOR

Over 60 years combined and we still keeping it tight
Became legends and founders with the history book in sight

My brother..... Fellow legend and founder of P.O.E.T
Thank you for that message and the love you been showing

TERRI L. JOHNSON

TERRI L. JOHNSON

TERRI L. JOHNSON

Born Terri Lynn Julie Johnson, a First Nations Cree woman from the Samson Cree Nation in Maskwacis, Alberta, Canada. Terri has been a member of the P.O.E.T Organization since 2011. She has been featured in Volume 1 of the P.O.E.T. Anthology: Closed Mics Don't Get Fed, Volume 2 of the P.O.E.T. Anthology. In December of 2012, Terri Received an Author's Award from the P.O.E.T. Organization for her efforts in her individual published works in 2012. She has also been featured on P.O.E.T. Radio with Blaq Ice from Chicago Illinois. She additionally was a featured poet in "A Poetically Spoken Anthology" and was also the very first featured poet of "The Year of the Poet" in January 2014, through Inner Child Press.

Terri has performed her poetry at "Strictly for the Listeners" open mic, in Chicago Illinois and many other venues throughout Canada and the United States. Terri has published 4 books of poetry and has been contributed in many anthologies. Terri's books can be found at Inner Child Press : www.innerchildpress.com and other retail outlets globally.

The Purging...the Breathing...the Essence of the Soul of Terri: Poetic expressions,
June 2011
Inner Child Press. Ltd.

Voices: First Nations
March of 2012
This book is an treatise of the voices of First Nations Peoples
Inner Child Press. Ltd.

The Warrior Within,
June 2014,
This book is a tribute book to the death of her late son Teagan Johnson, who was murdered through gang violence at the age of fifteen.
Inner Child Press. Ltd.

Deeper
December 2016
This book is a poetic examination of Terri's sensuality and eroticism.
Inner Child Press. Ltd.

Reality ~

Reality said he knew my pain,
He said your fading.
He said the pain is too much.
But I knew reality was wrong.
He knows nothing.
The pain was all we knew.
Evaded all thought.
Like a whisper,
Talking through our veins.
Yet no soothing for the ache.
Just more pain.
Reality lied and said,
We would be ok.
Watched our tears fall.
Made our suffering worse.
It kept us numb.
Kept us so hazed.
Pain sided with reality.
Yet we couldn't quite see it.
Formed a life on lies.
Made the bad just a fantasy.
A fantasy we couldn't see.
Too blind to all but now.
Truth is now just a memory.
Because reality fed me
What it needed to.
Fed us all the lies
Stifled all our cries.
Made it impossible,
Impossible to move on.
Fed our anger and guilt.
Made it all worse.
Reality was our pain,
Made me live in so much shame.
Now it's hurt that surrounds.

The life within my words ~

He was the life within my words.
My bloodline that made the ink flow.
My melody to my poetry.
Like honey so sweet.
The rhyme in his step called to me.
Sweeping me off my feet
and setting all the words free.
Touching me in ways,
Caressing me in erotic shades.
Not once letting the lust fade.
He stoked the fire in my verses
Made the rhymes flow so perfect.
The flow made me shake.
The melody that night he did take.
In sync we sang
Over and over again.
The life in my words
The poetry in my blood
that never blurred.

She once was ~

She wasn't feeling life
at the moment.
Things were just
not going right.
The craziness of days,
were building up.
So overflowing,
was the fill of her cup.
Nights were the worse,
where shadows clung deep.
Truths were a curse,
and made her soul to weep.
But still she woke
with tears that have gone dry.
Stuffing the fears inside,
wrapping herself within.
Walking aimlessly ahead.
No numbing clouding her head.
The overwhelming,
kept clawing.
Whispering deep inside.
So loud,
that most days,
she just wanted to hide.
Time and again,
she wanted to cry.
Day after day,
each tear had run dry.
Her heart was wrapping
itself in unforgivable stone.
Caring became nonexistent.
Life was mechanical.
Clouds became persistent.
The darkness was becoming
more comfortable.
Inviting her to nothing.

Inviting her not to care.
Inviting her to lose herself.
Caressing all her fears.
She was becoming someone else.
Some didn't recognize.
But then again,
the outside image
always sufficed.
Now a shadow of
what she once was.
It was all she could afford,
since life wasn't offering
Not much anymore.

Sinful hell ~

Tempting as I bite my lip.

Sweetness so thick.

So addictive

Like a possession.

Chaotically erotic

So damn seductive.

A sinful hell.

A passion

I want to yell.

I'm in anticipation,

Can't you tell...

The Change ~

The change was quick
no chance to hear the clock tick.
Too much time flew by.
Age so evident in clear light.
Mirrors showed a face,
I no longer knew.
Nor a specific moment
of a time or place.
Lost in heart.
Burdened so heavy in soul.
Buried myself time and again.
Covered in grief and shame.
So much denial
I did so much wrong.
Too much fog.
I couldn't find my way out.
My pain so heavy
I couldn't scream or shout.
I couldn't even stand to look at myself.
Tears no longer spilled
hate lived deep within.
Life no longer worked,
and dreams....
became a myth.

"I choose to speak life, I choose to live my life to my maximum potential, and I choose to celebrate my life."

MONICA GRAY

MONICA GRAY

MONICA GRAY

Monica Gray is a very talented and skilled writer, story teller and poet. She found her gift at an early age using her writings to express what she held deep inside her soul. The more she wrote the more powerful her pen became. Her pen became her voice and a way for her to break the silence. She became an honorary member of the P.O.E.T organization in 2016 and continues to grow in her gift. Be sure to look out for her in the future.

RISE SON RISE

Holding back the tears straining to see past this fog that's clouding me
Raindrops of fears that I'll never experience a love that mimics above. Studying to drown this doubt in me
Embracing the nature around me while hiding from the rain
Forcing Smiles on my face hoping to mask the pain
That's settled within my core
How long till I'm no longer sore
Or reminded of how much of myself was giving away
Only to be handed back with years of decay
These feelings are rough
I've been watered down enough
Rise Son rise, come down from the sky and shine on me

Each day I'm fighting not to lose the person I was created to be
Fog and clouds and rain storms doesn't Define who God is, neither do they define me
Remembering the promise of rainbows in the sky
That nothing I've been purposed to do is wrapped up in a guy
Who's was flawed and imperfect
My life is not worthless
As I have been made to feel by all the things he couldn't stand
Though now I see it only showed his lack of being a man
It's still tough
I've been held down long enough
Rise Son rise, come down from the sky and shine on me

Shield of Faith

There is Life in the battle
There is war on the field
Embracing life can be a challenge
when Battle Scars are not healed

The pain can lead to Armageddon
The joy it steals is real
Though other soldiers stand with you
they cannot tell how you feel

But there was a Balm in Gilead
that also lives in you
Who wants you to get to the rainbow
after the storm is through

He'll guide you through the minefields
without you being scathed
The enemy has already been defeated
when Jesus was raised from the grave

But so many times our eyes are tricked
in believing in what they see
That we live our lives from the battlefield,
instead of victory

So remember that Life is in the battle
Though war is on the field
Let Life be your reality
And Faith be your Shield

Joyful

Profound, wonderful, that's what He is to me.
I feel this way because today I stand in victory.
Not because of anything that I have said or done.
But simply by the Father's gift in giving us His Son.
Instead of seeing only thorns, roses are attached.
I'm viewing things from up above opposed to on my back.
Powerful hosts and heavenly rhythms are now guiding me through.
And though I know the world's the same, somehow all things look new.
The Royal King of everything saw fit to draw me in.
Then crown me with His Righteousness so true life can begin.
I wear my crown with confidence and never let it fall.
Staying full so I in turn can share this gift with all.
But if I lose my crown of proof, then who will hear my plea?
Listening ears are inclined to hear the voice of royalty.
I sit with Him upon the throne cause where He is, I am.
So glad to feel the presence of this precious Holy Lamb.

Beyond Me

I'm digging deeper to gain stability. Moving beyond my normal ability. Leaving the shallow water and sand. Hopping upon a cruise to new land. No burdensome baggage to wait on or claim. No childish behavior or silly love games. Got no time for liars and no room for cheats. Criteria for boarding is wholesome and sweet. I'm digging in deeper securing foundation. Hoping to dock my ship called "Relation". Explore possibilities of fertile soil. To plant my life with minimal toil. Enjoying green pastures besides still streams. Allowing my Shepherd to guide me and gleam. Deeply I'm digging so deeply indeed. To reap the harvest of The Holy Seed.
By Monica Renee

"Let your hard work be done in silence
and allow your success to make noise for you.
All you have to do is reap the benefits and stay
grounded in God's purpose for your life."

LADY JO

JoAnn Smith

LADY JO

JOANN SMITH AKA LADY JO

LADY JO was born JoAnn Smith, a native of Chicago and grew up in the Ida B. Wells project housing, in the mid 1960's. Being a shy little girl growing up, she was compelled to pick up her pen to express herself through her writings. This was due to a bad speech impediment. She was often misunderstood which led her to speak through her pen.

THE TEENAGE YEARS During her high school years, while attending Wendell Phillips high school in Chicago's Bronzeville neighborhood, she began to take writing seriously by taking journalism classes. Being impressed with her creativity, her journalism teacher, Ms. Dennings, encouraged her to write short stories. This was the turning point for LADY JO, it was then that she knew, others would take her writings seriously. Her cover stories would often be featured in the High School newspaper.

THE MAKINGS OF LADY JO As in adult, life began to divert her from her passion. She became the mother of two beautiful children. She would spend fifteen years away from writing, rearing her children. Although her children were the joy of her life, not being able to write left a void inside her soul. A family member and poet/saxophonist, Mellow J, invited her to an open mic poetry set that he hosted and her spirit became stirred inside. She would soon begin attending open mic poetry sets, which inspired her to return back to her first love and her passion for writing. In 2016, she saw a flier online promoting a poet cookout and decided to attend the event. Little did she know that this would be a life changing decision. She met Blaq Ice and the P.O.E.T. organization, an artist activist group based in Chicago, who uses it's art for activism work. Shortly after, she would join P.O.E.T and become a member, putting her right on the national stage, assuming the stage name LADY JO. She began speaking in front of thousands, performing at major events such as the BANTU FEST, the R.A.G.E. community concert and mentoring at several schools and community events. Later that year she would win the 2016 best up and coming P.O.E.T award, but this would only be the beginning.

NATIONAL AWARD WINNING POET In 2017 she would go on to win a NSWA (NATIONAL SPOKEN WORD AWARD) for best up and coming poet. With this book release, you can add the title PUBLISHED AUTHOR to her credit. LADY JO is an overcomer, conquering all these achievements while battling Lupus, a disease that affects the internal organs and Lichen Planus, a disease that affects the skin. She is a true super shero and an example to many who are dealing with the challenges of life. Her motto is, "If I can do it, anyone can."

FACEBOOK: JOANN SMITH
INSTAGRAM: STORMY.JS49

LADY JO

CLOSE YOUR EYES

When a drowned heart carries pain
Close your eyes, feel the breeze and see tall trees swaying, swaying to the tune of the rustling winds
Close your eyes
Go to a place that never stops, a tranquil place where waterfalls cascade to the mountain's edge
Hear whispers of sweet nothings and let the smell of roses fills your nostrils,
Close your eyes
Imagine tantalizing touches
Think indefinable thoughts until the thrill of love has rested in the pit of your stomach
Close your eyes
Feel the trickling rain that glows your skin and
See the crescent moon as the virtuous sound of a comforting voice flutters the air
Close your eyes think deep thoughts when your heart is drowned
And there you will find the rarity of a best friend that eclipses your heart giving fruits that feed your mind

WHAT'S ON MY MIND

Life is not long five twenties' is all we get, one for play or should I say for discovery and play then half way through the bulb goes off its two and one half telling us to stop but some will say I still got time
There is no time
What's on my mind is that,
We live in a nation full of haters a down low nation that is full of crocks and villains leaders that shouts democracy but in reality a dangerous game of constitutional stupidity. Governmental corruption that gang press our voices; and dismantle our votes with an indirect election called the Electoral College
What's on my mind
Hearts betray, the sword don't lie, and the best of fruit are rotting from the inside out let's aluminate light and extinguish the fire of hate
What's on my mind
We are melting like wax, turning to ashes doing to us what slavery could not do lets stop the abstraction of not only brothers but generation children that will not be born because of shots to back
Look at our prisons they are stacked, packed and full of blacks who are told and controlled with a dedicated pace
What's on my mind
On enemy grounds we stand
Please understand that the aspiration of the enemy is banality, to wipe us out so let's not contribute to the explosions of inhumane slaughter of our own people
What's on my mind is that we live in a nation where being black is their means to attack and at the end of the day the line is blocked the blue is protected and at the end of the day, they go stack their lies and disguise them as truths and the black man's theme is still I can't breathe
Look at our nation a nation of lies that tell us to vote, and then go and work a laborious job for laborious pay. Work to be paid, get paid to pay bills then pay to go on vacation and get docked for being sick.
Tongues of murder complex codes twisted words
Look at our nation

LADY JO

UNDER SIEGE

There is an epidemic of homicides that's sieging our souls we cannot stroll on a warm summer day because of shots to the back

Summer is loathed winter a reprieve from the smoking guns and blaring sires corner stores are morgues obliteration is the norm,

There is never a dull moment every day is like the Fourth of July, and late in the night the death toll rise

People are dying left and right, dying at night for rolling the dice

Its death and destruction the killings keep coming

Mothers are screaming because life is a struggle a cycle of trouble and all too often son souls are sold then traded up for white gold, white lies and demise is it the sign of the times

Oh, how dreary that the reality of death is worse than life

Tormented in sleep by the iniquities of the street we hope for the best but prepare for worst

Tired and afraid surrounded by despair emerged in madness, muted lips and closed eyes keep us alive

Contained by fear and tamed with shame that we hide in plain sight pretending not to see the gun casing and dime bags that litter the streets and like blotted art blood decorates the streets

The perpetual killings, the furry of revenge leaves everlasting flames of hurt and pain I don't understand

It makes me teary that a child of five wave their hands and continue to play at the sound of shots and when left alone will wonder for blocks and find dead bodies in empty lots.

From east to west and soon after dusk bright lights from the sky seep through tall trees, brush across buildings from low flying copters that circle the skies as blaring sirens race in the night to save a life.

And still a mother cries because all she sees is two dead eyes looking in hers praying for her demise

YESTERDAY

Yesterday I looked at you

Your hands reached

Your toes wiggled

Your eyes glowed

At times, you stared

I often wonder

If you saw

Today

WHERE DID YOU GO

The tree was up
The lights flickered
The snow floated to the earth
When you left I searched for you,
At the park
At grandma's house
I even looked under the bed for you
Where did you go?
Many days I inquired of you
Why did you leave?
No good bye, no see you later
You just left
Honest answers I did not get
I thought you flew away
In the closet
In the basement under tables is where I looked
For sure, I thought you would return
Where did you go?
I looked for you in the skies
In my dreams I looked for you
I looked, I looked, and I looked for you
You should have known I would search
Quick and sudden you departed
All you did was, fly away
No one cared about my tears
No one cared that my heart bled for you
Because all you did was, fly away

THE ENDURER

Anthony L. Briscoe

THE ENDURER

THE ENDURER

Born Anthony L. Briscoe - The Endurer is a Spoken Word artist in Chicago that infuses a plethora of life experiences to reach the young people in the City of Chicago. He is a veteran of the United States Armed Forces, an ordained minister, and currently serves as a technologist in Chicago Public Schools.

He is a native of Chicago and an aspiring motivational speaker within local school communities and has addressed youth in small and large group settings throughout the Chicagoland area due to his creative methods of urging youth to rise above their circumstances and champion success. He is a published devotional writer for the Apostolic Church of God who has written professionally for corporations such as Boeing International and the Noble Network of Charter Schools. He is a budding photographer capturing many events on the poetry scene in Chicago and works actively with the C.H.A.M.P.S mentoring program.

The Endurer is proof that hardship at a young age does not determine your future. His goal is to see men and young people break free from childhood pain and bondage and walk free in the liberty that he has found in Jesus Christ.

The Endurer can be found at his blog, tonybriscoe.co

THE ENDURER

He Got Us

Jesus, help me pick up the pieces of my life I
Lost my connection to you just like my wifi
People judging me while a log is in their eye, Lord why-why

Hurting myself sometimes it just runs through my mind
But I'm not ready to tell this world goodbye bye
Especially if I won't see you when I die, Lord, I cry cry

Lift me up now, on my knees screaming out from pain pain
Holding on the to power in your name name
I'll lose it all if in you I'll know I'll gain gain
You died for me rose again from the Bloodstain

If I can get through the pressure of these self-doubts
My mental illness and the battle of these tough bouts
Drive my psyche through the trail of these rough routes
Rebuke the enemy, I'm too great, he wants me snuffed out

Are you there? Can you hear me? Please respond
I'm hurting, I need healing, where's my balm?
I really do not want to cause myself harm
My friends tell me just to keep calm, they missed the alarm

My child, I'm with you, I'm not your parents or your girl I won't quit you
I'm not the bullies in the hood, I'll never hit you
When you trouble I won't split I'll come and get you
When you're depressed I'll lift you up, won't let him sift you

Stand by your side, I will never Judas kiss you
There's not a job that you can't do I will equip you
There is nothing you can do to make resent you
Satan accuses you but knows I represent who (you)

To come at you, you know he needs my consent to
Just to ensure that it's me you commit to
Take your meds, give no reason to commit you
I'll never leave or forsake my blood is thick too

My Holy Spirit dwells within my love is stick to
When you're travailing in your prayer my power kicks too
Express yourself in written bars my Spirit spits too
Let it rip through cause, child I hear you!

THE ENDURER

Seeds

I am here again, because this is familiar,
My desk, my chair, my work, my office has been refuge
The kids are there, and you are there, but it is no longer home
It is a strange place because we are no longer familiar
We are broken objects in the shadows of a forgotten relationship
A memory of a love that once flourished is now vanishing
With figments of an imaginative foreign substance called……regret

We don't exist in this realm of emotions; we only share a space that is dead

Daddy, I miss you, I miss you too little princess
When are you coming home, I'm waiting for you

Tears stream from the loss of my seed; it has been years since I have seen them
All they know if that daddy takes care of them
I have abandoned their hearts with a check book

What happened to our love, how could it be so easily disturbed?
Shattering the dreams of those that said "I want to be like them"
They are like us, following our example of divorce, men have left their wives
And women have left their husbands for self-aggrandizement
And the seeds of the forgotten are forever with us
Dismembered, screaming, in agony as they now refused to settle down

The sting of divorce has left them
unable to trust
unable to dream
unable to commit
unable to love
unable to endure
unable to hope

It has become oh, too familiar

Lingering

If he looked into your soul
He would see a secret that only you knew
You'll gage his eyes and realize
This is love, this is meant to be

In you lies a mystery of intrigue
A question with no answer
A foundation with no source
A road with no course

The journey calls for you
It echoes off the corners of your heart
Purpose wrestles with fear
Destiny wars with doubt

Trying to entertain your worth
You shudder to think of three years from now
At this time, you grab the moment
Seize the day, appreciate the current

You respond to the image of night suns
That paint silhouettes across northern skies
You count the stars and envision a gift
A seed that has been implanted into your psyche
You awake and find serenity in the stillness of time
Yawning with arms stretched out you huge yourself
Smiling, you move closer to the inner you and whisper
"I love you girl"

If he looked into your soul
He would see a secret that only you know
You'll gage his eyes and realize
This is love, this is meant to be

THE ENDURER

Frozen

It feels like months
Where have I traveled?
A place of mystery and uncertainty
I can't believe I am here
In this place, at this moment
Thinking, relishing, questioning
My purpose, my call, my existence
Surrounded but alone
Clinging to hope yet untethered
Trapped in the crevices of thought
I've traveled here before
It's uncomfortable, that face, the reflection
Its shadow reaching out to hug me
Whispers of I love you, you have a purpose
You exist for a reason
I don't embrace it I turn off the light
Tears run down the mirror
I've been here before, it hasn't been days
It's been hours
In front of an empty table
Food cold, coffee bland, water lukewarm
Depression says hello

Father's Day

I grew up around the Elders
They became fathers when dad failed us
There were times when anger swelled us
Hating the men we looked like overwhelmed us

Times were frustrating full of pretending and phony
Mom was struggling and sometimes we went hungry
Not a lot of friends' times were lonely
Buster Browns and Tough Skins were on me so I looked homely

Friends playing catch with their dad and I asked God where's mine
Broken on the inside, outside pretending to be fine
Wonder if he thought of me, I just wanted a little of his time
Where's the man that would groom me to see, I felt blind

Starting seeing many women, never faithful in my flirt
My drug dealing, gang banging, strip clubs, and all my dirt
But God spoke in the midst of all my hurt
Said you've tried everything, but only I work

Stopped in my tracks, in the midst of the tears
Could I truly be a man with no man to hold dear
Could grow up and start to see things clearer
Get over my fear and love this face in the mirror

He said son you can, I'll empower you with my Holy Spirit
He'll teach you how to be a man
See I know your father ran but the Holy Spirit will teach you to stand
Engage yourself in my word and learn my commands
I'll tap into your gift and empower you to take the land

One word, one rhyme, one child at a time
But it starts with you having a Christ-like mind
Seek after me and destiny you will find
Just stay dormant for a while so I can help you unwind

THE ENDURER

See your father was broken just like you
And the reason is that his father was broken too
Give your life to me and I will remake ya
You'll be the curse breaka
And everything the Enemy meant for bad I'll turn for your good
I'll raise you up as an example right in the hood

I'll take you beyond the best you can be
Snatch them corporate shackles off your feet and set you free
So you can be the leader I've created you to be
So your sons and daughters will see my power in thee

I'll send a servant that teaches the truth of my gift
I'll send a pastor that will free you from hells rift
I'll surround you with men that love their wives
Men that trust God and pay their tithes
Men that, for you, will lay down their lives
Men that let you know they are hurt and won't wear a disguise

Men that will stand up against the wiles of the devil
Men that will teach you to humility no matter what level
Men that will empower you to hold up your chest
To keep your chin up in failure if you did your best

And I'll bring your father back into your life
Put those shattered bones back together that were broken by strife
Everything wrong, I'll make it right
And on his death bed, you'll have no regrets because I made it tight

I am the Father, when no one else bothered
When you ran the streets, I kept you from the slaughter
I am the Father, when you chose the wrong men
I protected your daughter
When you turned your back on me, I just smiled
Not even you can jump out of my hand once you're my child

I am the Father, humble yourself at my feet
Hear my word wayward dads, you no longer have to be a dead beat
Man up, go back to that child you've neglected
Ask for forgiveness, let them know in me you've been resurrected

Repent for all those years you rejected and neglected
Endure their pain and you being disrespected
And watch the chains fall off
Watch me make their stony heart soft
Trust my word and see
That I'll make every day a Father's Day with me

"Sometimes you got to step out by blind faith to do something that you have never done before."

MZ. NINA

Nina A Calloway

MZ. NINA aka NINA A. CALLOWAY

MZ. NINA AKA NINA A. CALLOWAY

Nina was conceived by Gertrude Calloway, and Marshall Calloway born on June 15, 1969 at 3:31 am in Cook County hospital, under the sign "Gemini". Interesting enough her personality traits identify very closely with what astrology experts call "Character Identifiers". Jovial, loving, loyal, analytical, emotional, ambitious, fickle-minded, easily board, talented, and unattracted to smothering people and/or situations. However, to have in your life is a blessing.

Her love for the arts especially dancing began at the innocent age of 11; her experience is extensive. The first time she performed in front of a live audience was at church, where she tapped-danced for her Easter Program, she was astoundingly amazing; after the program was over the choir director requested an encore performance for the late commers.

That is the experience that piloted her career; Ogden Park Field House on 65th & Racine, Joseph Holmes Dance School, GMG Dancers Incorporated, American Boyz & Girls Dance Ensemble, Disco Steppers, and the ACOG Liturgical Dance Ensemble are the professional dance organizations which trained her in various forms of the art of dance.

Tap, Ballet, Hip/Hop, Liturgical (Praise Dancing), and Modern Jazz are the styles of Dance that make up her profile over the 39 years, and she is currently still performing. She has encountered many setbacks in this life. Her experiences were necessary to bring her to the woman she become today.

Through dance she can be expressive without uttering a word; it's her gift, her peace beyond this world. Art to me is effortlessly natural, it's a form of expression where boundaries are none; until this very day she still dances with grace, poise, and dedication.

MZ. NINA aka NINA A. CALLOWAY

Speaking 2 U "Without Words"

Through the movements of my hands I give you direction; controlling vision, to where your eyes are fixed; such control that your motion of blinking turns into a stare. Thoughts of pure peace began to calm your mind where acceptance of my control is now evident, because you are attuned with the experience of communicating without words.

The ability to express various emotions weather pain, pleasure, happiness or sadness; in my world I communicate messages WITHOUT WORDS, I only have the responsibility of ensuring that I've spoken to you in a way only interpretive to you.

Though my body, has an entirely different language, it can be translated as a calm storm, a tornado that doesn't cause damage; but the beautiful sunshine after the storm; yes, you can sit through my performance, be entertained, and take the experience with you for the rest of your life.

Dance is what I do to bring you into a place of peace without words, but the experience that you encounter is your interpretation to take with you, for the rest of your life.

My life purpose is my gift, my gift is D.A.N.C.E. (Drawing, Audiences Near to Calming Experiences)

My Wisdom

I was gifted with a blessing beyond measure
It was my pleasure to bring into the world
A beautiful baby girl who actually gave me life
I named her Wisdom Darrianna Wright

From her grandmother to her mother
She had some strong spiritual teachers
She has become a true manifestation of her name,
She is a very wise and strong Libra

She has a very calm nature
She loves Jesus, her Lord and Savior
And her name was given to me by the Holy Spirit
She listens to the word
Whenever she hears it

Very open minded to receive knowledge
With aspirations to go to college
She takes high school very series
She's on both the wrestling
And debate/speech teams
At Harold L. Richards

Her skin has this beautiful red skin tone
But she's not a red bone
She's a beautiful mixture of African American
And native Indian Cherokee
A perfect blend of her dad and me

D.A.N.C.E.

No matter the sound, I can adapt to my environment; the only thing I need is space, and a place to move freely, illustrate, and construct the desired results for interpretation. Actually sound isn't necessary its an accessory needed only for added entertainment. My choreography stem from my deepest thoughts, bringing my dreams to reality; I dance methodically, physical expressions of my emotions, and life experiences, I'm a master of D.A.N.C.E. it's who I am, when I'm communicating without words. So I welcome life as she comes and gives the greatest lessons, my only response is to D.A.N.C.E because Destiny Always Needs Creative Expression

P.O.E.T. ANTHOLOGY VOLUME VI

"Tough people outlast tough times."

BRAZEN

Rakeiaa Fortner

BRAZEN aka RAKEIAA FORTNER

BRAZEN AKA RAKEIAA FORTNER

March 25, 2011, the POET family came to Chicago Woodlawn charter and changed my life forever. POET provided me with a platform that I used for self-healing and change. In that class, I sat under a table and wrote. When I got home later that night I continued writing. My first piece would later be entitled PTSD, furthermore, it described the adversities I had faced in battling this syndrome, and how poetry helped me to take control of my own PTSD. In this mentoring program hosted by POET, Brazen was born. Bold and without shame, I personified every bit of my poet name. I went on to join the POET family and perform all over Chicago, and eventually internationally in Australia. I took my passion with me to college and continued to organize events and perform at my school and at local churches in the community. What started as a mentoring program in high school, evolved into my passion.

BRAZEN AKA RAKEIAA FORTNER

My Journey

"Pumpkin" my grandmother said in a tone that I had never heard her use. A tone that was so dark and depressing I could not find pleasure in it. "Your mother was really sick, and she passed away today." Everything from that moment went black, I couldn't feel, hear, or see anything. As if trapped inside cages in my mind that I had never been in before. I had no control over the actions my body made. I was emotionally numb; my heart had no feeling but pain. It felt as if death came to my door just to take my heart away and leave me with nothing but an empty rib cage. I felt each and every one of my grandmother's words cut through my chest and shoot through my heart only to stay and act as a time bomb waiting to blow. My mind was non-existent because heaven abducted it somewhere between my grandmas first and last words. No longer able to serve me any good. My heart was no longer protected. No longer able to live in complete happiness but as if poisoned with those words it laid there sick, beat up, and in need of medical treatment. It was no longer strong or bright red, it no longer served as my strength but now as my biggest burden and weakness.

When I was seven years old my mother passed away from Sickle Cell Anemia. A blood disease that occurs when two people with sickle cell trait conceives a child. Fortunately, my Grandparents: Willie lee Fortner and Queen Esther Fortner, and my uncle, Gaston Fortner, stepped in to raise my brother and I. My oldest brother Rashad Fortner graduated at 16, went away to college, and caught a case that incarcerated him for ten years. The system failed my brother and took away ten years of our time together. We had no idea our time would be cut so short. Due to the traumatic experiences of my childhood I was diagnosed with Post trauma A blood disease that occurs when two people with sickle cell trait conceives a child.

In high school I became a student ambassador and traveled the world: Australia, Canada, Jamaica, Bahamas, etc. During these travels I realized just how divided but equally oppressed diasporic- black people have become. It occurred to me that the only solution would be Pan- Africanism, the uniting of all black and brown people in the world. I started performing Spoken word Poetry as a defense against oppression across the diaspora. My senior year of high school my father passed away; however, I didn't get discouraged I continued to travel, perform, and spreads my new vision. I created a flower crown business called "Crown Me Queen" wear I sold floral crowns in black communities. Have you ever handed a young black girl a crown and said, "You are a Queen," My belief is that words pack powerful meaning, and flower crowns aligned with those words symbolizes strength and self-esteem. My business plan got me a scholarship and into the NFTE Entrepreneur semi-finals competition.

I chose to go away to Knox College in Galesburg to study Neuroscience; however, they weren't interested in having black math and science graduates, so, they used my literary skills to place me as a lit major. I used this misfortune to my advantage. Since I had more time not studying science, I began performing in all Galesburg predominantly white Churches. Now you may ask what good does it do to preach about your oppression to the ancestors of the oppressors? I believe there is nothing more enslaved than the minds of the oppressor. The ideology of supremacy is toxic and poisons the brains of Caucasians just like institutionalization poisons blacks. We have to make this "uncomfortable" subject more openly discussed and fought against. Knox College did not like the organizing of the black student body and eventually punished me for my efforts. Eventually my grandma fell very ill in the hospital, forcing me to come home and leave my fight against Knox county, but my message was clear and lived on. Grandma died and rose again after a week, and, she has gained all of her mobility and speech back with the work of her family and God.

January 30, 2018 my brother was killed in a car truck collision. I say this to say the devil will not stop attacking you. Satin will never stop taking your peace, taking your joy, and attempting to take your ability to love yourself and others. With the strength of God, I was able to overcome the adversities in my life and commit them to paper.

BRAZEN AKA RAKEIAA FORTNER

Chicago Change Gone Come

Chicago the Windy City, Wear bullets fly Like Planes.
My Brother shot one in the sky and yelled his name, praying, "God Hear Me!"
Death is in the seams.
Politicians push for poverty, they prey you shoot for lesser means.
Shoot for incarceration.
Brotherhoods turned gangs; we're shooting for acceptation.
Claiming you own the block but in denial with your claims 'cause,
The white man has the key to the city and copyrights to your last name.
Damn, it feels like a sea we're lost
Obama said "We Can" but didn't realize the boat was rocked
Like how you can perform for inauguration
Then weeks later get gunned down while playing in the park
Friends frantically feel for bullet wounds while the light of your life goes dark.
What's the price of a black woman's heart?
Commoditized, cut open, left lifeless and frozen,
Awaiting her mother to find what's left of her body parts.
You wonder why it's been; so many amber alerts,
Black Queen's gone missing lately?
You turn on the news and don't see the FED's investigating.
Well let me explain, this is what happens when you don't push for change.
Complacently called a Modern-Day Slavery.
Too raise a child it takes a village we should all be ashamed.
While those that make it out try and remain estranged,
Bullets wetting kids like water in the rain.
Poor babies never got to know change.
It's time to make a difference!
Melt all the guns into armor let's assume the position.
I dream of Oppression being buried alive,
A million men marching solely for Black Lives.
Set up 50 detours shut down the whole Lake Shore drive.
Black baby girls are going to look in the mirror and see nothing but self-love.
This city is crying tangible tears of blood,
And, we can no longer wait for change to come.

I AM SICK

God, so I don't usually do this thing, but whoever you may be.
Tangible or intangible please
Reach your hands out to me because I don't have a clue
Caught at the cross roads of adversity and I don't know what to do.
God! I am sick.
Not physically, but mentally, emotionally of all the wrongs that I see in my community.
 I am sick
Sick of my people bragging about the ghetto
When the ghetto is a situation we should be trying to get out of.
I guess that's why it's called a trap.
Products of ignorant people and un-conscience rap.
God did not give us life for us to keep it still.
We're supposed to keep moving and progressing
So why are my people still stuck here, in the ghetto?
As if chained to the bottom so we can never rise to the top.
We are victims, victims of the street.
Instead of running we are skipping so we start to skip beats,
Beats like how Enslaved Africans were beaten and oppressed,
And, now those same struggles hide behind lyrics said by rappers in ignorance.
Oppression like, how we were conned into turning against each other and now we turn against each other without the help of anyone.
Helpless like, what they did to us back then;
Separating are families forcefully, and, now are families are separate because these young boys were never taught to be young men.
This is the ghetto
And I am sick
I am sick of teenage girls making babies before making honor role.
We came from Kings and Queens but now aren't even honorable
I am tired of Obama being our youth's only positive influence.
Trading your innocence, no common sense, to ignorance.
 I'm sick of this miss perception of cool this is the birth of a nation overpopulated with fools.
I'm sick of Australians being painted as white when the first inhabitants were aboriginals whose skin was closer to black like Egyptians in Africa Native Americans in America and Mexicans in Mexico at least before these nations were attacked.

BRAZEN AKA RAKEIAA FORTNER

Why is it that everywhere the oppressor went he bore tragedy and sickness and now he's looked at as pure, and innocent and why are my people trying to resemble him through self-hatred?
I'm sick of people thinking that slavery doesn't affect the present day like we don't still show and continue to follow those same traits.
I pray to God he is my spinach he gives me strength.
I internalized his message and scream my thoughts out on stage.
I dream of an educated and powerful race, but dreams are illegal in the ghetto.
They say children are whipped to do rite, but we've been whipped to stand back and do wrong.
And who ever said they got rid of Jim Crow laws?
This is not me.
I will not let society define me I am a queen.
Born from Africa and Nefertiti I am the dominant and original being
I am the mother of the earth, and the strongest of the herd.
God gave me the gift of my voice so I bless the world with my words.
I kiss the sky when it snows.
I leave crowds in shivers because my words are ice cold.
I am a gift and to the world I gave birth,
But the father is hatred and bloody segregation.
That explains the chaos we now call earth
For centuries good and evil remained balanced,
But lately I've been sick and keeping equality is a challenge.
I fight and I fight but my body continues to hurt.
All that I'm left to do is grow sicker while watching my world get worse.
Mother Nature is sick

Dear Mama,

When my mom was pregnant with me they thought she'd die in labor; but, the delivery was a success, and, my mom was happy she gave birth to her first daughter.
I'd like to apologize for the stress I've caused.
I can't imagine what it's like to wake up with death and baby in arm.
Asking God how'd I make it this far?
Then have to barricade the exits with bricks and boards.
Cause the grim reaper keeps knocking on the back door.
Why was my baby born so premature?
With IV's for limbs and heart monitors for cries.
I hear her beeping in the incubator and I'm too weak to dry her eyes.
Dear Mama,
I apologize for your heart beat that bleed in C notes.
The sickle cell crisis wear you yelled like mothers at the sight of C-sections.
The nights wear you and I both lay restless
Because your body was attacking you from the inside
If only I wasn't too young to realize are days together were numbered.
Every tea party, snow angel, pageant crumbled and swallowed into the earth.
You could have been saved.
All it took was mere research.
But black folks are the only ones sickle cell hurt.
Stop I can't breathe is much deeper than you think.
We're not just being executed/ exterminated in the streets.
Medical advancement is stagnant.
Stiffening smiles stifling over complex statements forged in fraud.
Needles 33 to 7 gauge burst and inflame you veins.
While apathetic doctors kept shooting until your eyes would roll away.
I saw your face pour down with rein.
I wonder if your mind ever escaped the flaming pains your body consumed.
If you found peace at heavens gates knowing you didn't die at 2, 22,
Or and time doctors wrongfully assumed.
Dear Mama,
You are so far beyond measure or factor.
Willis tower envied your heights and stature.
Your beauty was like treasure.
Black woman lives matter!
No picture could capture your true essence and heart.

BRAZEN AKA RAKEIAA FORTNER

You held the family up and shielded us like Noah's Ark.
Now my thoughts have gone dark.
With the same pain that haunted you for years
I look in the mirror.
I see your face.
I shed the same tears.
Silently suffering sleep deprivation.
Swollen with Sorrow and too late to say.
Dear Mama,
This is my appreciation.

Ye'

Slavery a Choice, I can't help but take offense.
As if we chose to get extracted and loaded up on ships.
My mother died waiting on an assist,
From doctors more focused on the color of her skin.
Ignorance is an abyss that takes you.
My worst enemy is ignorance, but I still can't hate you.
You isolated anything hereditarily relevant to you.
Left it spiritually starving and dying off with your bleach dyed roots.
You tried to kill the soil, didn't you?
You colored your eyes a similar blue
As the waters that carried the babies of African enslaved mothers.
Who clutched their own children and jumped overboard.
They foresaw their own doom.
Enslaved Africans were beaten and oppressed.
Now you mock these struggles with rhythmic ignorance.
Its bittersweet right?
Bittersweet how you can sit with elevated but shackled feet.
Using your culture for fame for you it's all a scheme.
What you forgot you're from Chicago?
50 bodies can drop in a week.
You think mothers choose to pour their hearts out and grieve.
Have their own wombs leaked into half apathetic streets.
Chyna Lions life was lost weeks before her graduation and prom.
My city is purging me.
And the reality cuts deep, deep like surgery.
You get to choose where your history begins and ends.
Man I'm still losing sleep over dying friends.
You thought you could buy back your 40 acres and reality TV got in the way.
Was the opioids and Lipo-suction to please Kim K?
Wow Kim-ye that life has scripted your soul to shame.
I have no negative twitter backlash.
Just sorrow for the day you see the remains of your garden.
An empty vase with no flowers just hallowed self-hate.
You said they make us hate ourselves and love they wealth.
On the road to riches and diamond rings.
Your living the American dream in discontentment.

BRAZEN AKA RAKEIAA FORTNER

I reference your lyrics because you are your own worst contradiction.
Now my own sleep deprivation got me up late listening to Kanye's old hit list.
He put his heart and soul into this business now his minds doing time in prison.
They say the people highest up have the lowest self-esteem.
So what about you?
Standing center stage deemed to mentally incompetent to speak the truth.
I guess these days you just up late nights shouting, "shoop-tidy Whoop".

Press and Curl

I heard this girl say she hates the thick fullness of her hair.
I looked around and told her
Baby that's your soul and what's left of a golden heir
Like heirs to the throne
We lead revolutions.
The thick full haired Haitians
Took their freedom alone,
But that's not written in America's theme song.
We still in the year 2018 choose to clap and sing along.
Dance as they continue to enslave us to systematic oppression
We ain't left the field at all.
We still look through Eurocentric lenses
We don't love ourselves at all.
But self- hate drove my brother to kill his own
And hate leads these officers to kill so many of my own.
America just doesn't seem like a place for me to call home.
But, don't get me wrong, if I didn't love it I wouldn't be here.
So watch me find reparations in my heart and in the knowledge of it all.
Next time I saw this girl she had a perm, a year later she cut it all off.
Press
I hate the way the media tries to control beauty
Quite frankly,
We have black men as dark as me
Trying to Americanize their image
Saying they wouldn't date a girl as dark as me
Or damn bae you pretty, damn bae you pretty,
To be a dark skin girl!
Crushed and enslaved under images of what it means to be beautiful
In white supremacist world
What does it mean that my brother's mothers are black?
Grandmothers that raised them
Gave them roots as rich as soil
But in sin
We still sit under the master
Trying to be more like him
Like how we can idolize images of a god drawn to look more like him

BRAZEN AKA RAKEIAA FORTNER

When in actuality Jesus traveled through Babylon and Egypt in Africa
Let's be honest he was more Afrikan
And now my brothers and sister both have been condemned
Crushed and crucified strange fruit
Maybe it's because we resemble him
Maybe we've taken these blows as a sacrifice like him
And my brothers and sisters need to realize we will always rise just like him
Trying to move forward when your back has been whipped
Hung by our necks
Beat with shotgun buts in the white man's grip
Death isn't always this good
It will leave you thirsty and starving running from master in the woods
Walking in Ferguson to be shot down and publicly displayed in the hood
And what do you think this means for a people psychologically
I just gave you 300 years of America's favorite hobby
And they say slavery doesn't still exist
But still in the year 2018 along with all this
Press
Imma tell you your worth
The blood in your veins is more righteous than church
The color of your skin serves as the proof of your strength
So brothers love yours, own your struggle, and have faith
I won't sit around and let oppression eat at my feet
No I'm not scared of change
Yeah I will walk through Birmingham, bare foot, and police force at bay.
I will make revolution a hot topic
Know my history and my name
Have pride in yourself
We can make freedom rein
Activism is merely taking a stand vs. standing around
Black is beautiful
Black is powerful
And for that I am proud
Press

P.O.E.T. ANTHOLOGY VOLUME VI

POETIC RAIN

POETIC RAIN

POETIC RAIN

Poetic Rain started writing poetry to make people happy. At 6 years old she admired the wordplay of Dr. Seuss and how it made her happy. She would write poems for everyone that read to her. She saw their insecurities and heard how they talked down to themselves. For birthdays she would have poems that were 1 or 2 stanzas long and design cards to show appreciation. Once she was introduced to Spoken Word her passionate side was replaced with a more understanding side.

She was the first person from her high school to perform poetry with the Chicago Symphony Orchestra. She bought into the program because she was a co-founder of two poetry groups known as The Black Angels and Lyrical Legends. While working with CSO, a woman who played the viola suggested she used the cadences of the music to help with her impact while performing.

Poetic Rain/Silent Storm - Is who she become on stage. Poetic Rain is the young woman who lets her heart bleed, whether it be about uplifting, acknowledging past hurt, embracing the joy of her sexuality or any form of love, for both self and others. Rain falls freely, and as she continues to grow, she wants the world to begin to flow with her.

Weakness

I'm tired of dealing with people that think they make me feel weak

From their repetitive standards

To their pasty faces

And false promises of growth

Being true to the truth is all that ever mattered to me

I don't give a damn about anyone's name or excuse

Everyone who decided not to push themselves is dead to me

I've had too many snakes try to break bread with me

But I always knew what sick sad thing sat in their heads

Weakness

I'm tired of dealing with people that think they make me feel weak

Because I'm strong

And their doubt of my ability is beneath me

Numb

They say we all keep secrets
Some die with us
But this secret has me truly confused
Before there was a stone in my chest
You kept me warm
Now I feel cold from the core
It seems as though the chill you left me with is seeping through
Everyone seems to see through
Making me feel transparent whether or not if I choose transparency
From my inner light burning bright
To the shadow looming deep inside me
Who am I when the lights are dim?
The camera flashes can't capture an essence of a being
So I leave my essence in the presence I'm in
Who am I when you leave?
Alone
Lonely and longing for the person you once were to me
Before you
I was alone
When I was alone
I felt numbness
Now I hurt
I'd give anything to feel numb again

Break the Box

Why do we become numb to the lack of self expression
We ain't ever been cool with being in the box
Yet we get older and want our kids to live in one
Good grades
College
Career
And what
A family to get good grades, college, career, and a family to get
Good grades
College
You get it
Can't miss it
Why do we act like we find peace in repetition?
That's basic
And we're beyond it
We're astounding
Yet for some reason we settle for the simplistic
We are divine
We could be creating things far beyond what's been seen
But we aspire to sit in cubicles and hide behind cash registers and other things
Innovation has become devoted to things instead of societal growth
We are just making more stuff just to make stuff to have
What have we done to the minds of our youth by giving them high speed content but keeping the quality low
They are filling their brains with nonsense
And then they express it aggressively because they haven't had real connections
Our economy is making anything below first class desperate
And I'm tired of packing my grocery cart looking pathetic

"If" Translated For The Youth

If you can focus on who you are and not what people make you out to be
If you can believe in your ability and still push through knowing others may rightfully disbelieve what you're able to do
If you can grow and not rush the natural process of growing
If you can be lied about and let knowing the truth guide how you move forward instead of feeding into the lies
If you can be hated for simply being who you are, do not react with more hate because that will lower you
If you can do all this without thinking you are above these things
If you can aspire and not feel incomplete without your aspirations
If you can think with purpose instead of doing it just to say it's been done
If you can remain humble in the same ways whether you win or lose
If you can hear what you've said twisted into lies to deceive others who believe in you having an ill nature

If you can make success and have to start completely over without hesitation and no support
If you can start over without needing to address who you use to be
If you have worked tirelessly towards a dream that you are starting to see the light dimming for but never actually give up
If you can code switch but still stand by your views
If you can hang with the high and mighty without breaking your code of conduct
If no individual person or circumstance can take your happy and reason to live away
If you can stay true to who you have been naturally to be with or without the support of others
If you can push your hardest to make a change or stand your ground, knowing you may lose your life but it can save someone else in the process
You will die a hero
A martyr
True to self and your beliefs
As a King or Queen of peace
Which is the highest honor bestowed upon a Man or Woman in their coming of age

Exposed

My brain is a labyrinth
The further you go the more dangerous I seem
Everyday is a game of chess
And I'm always 3 steps ahead
I'm looking for the king across the board
I'm taking the game
And ending it fast
But the more I play
The more I start to see my weaknesses
I falter at the thought of confrontation
I procrastinate like it's my greatest trade
Which is stupid
I am amazing
Beyond the setbacks that I've made
I have developed intricate plots
Enticed the most encrypted minds
And still had time to watch my shows

LADY DI

Diana Coatney Lewis Craig

LADY DI

LADY DI AKA
DIANA COATNEY LEWIS CRAIG

Diana Coatney Lewis Craig. Born on October 17, 1976 in Blue Island, Illinois to the proud parents of Priscilla and William Coatney. Educated in the south suburban school district of Robbins/Posen, Illinois. Her hobbies included oil pastel painting, swimming and collecting teddy bears. In college she majored in Early Childhood Education and minored in Art at Chicago State University. She attended Lewis University receiving a bachelor's degree in Criminal & Social Justice. Her memberships include P.O.E.T an acronym for People Of Extraordinary Talent under the direction of President Mr. Hawthorne and Vice President Mrs. Hawthorne. Sorority Lambda Kappa Mui. Temple of God Global Ministries, under the direction of Apostle Joyce Farmer. Also, she volunteers at the William Leonard Public Library in Robbins Illinois where the Director Library Administrator assists her with designing curriculum for youth programs and helps with government grant writing. As an independent business owner of MACFAB an acronym for "Making A Business For A Company," the music management client is classical, soprano Shawna Lewis, "A SYMPHONY." As a music manager her greatest accomplishment was booking the Chicago Bulls vs Cleveland Cavaliers, November 10, 2018 national anthem singer before the start of the basketball game. Her travels include Bahamas, St. Thomas, Puerto Rico, and Dominican Republic. As a business consultant she has connected major business moguls in conference type settings to Board Meetings.

THE NARCISSIST

Falling in love with lust agony pain tears with fears, when he met me, I was broken hearted. He crazy glued my heart back together. Thanks for the wine and dine. All the right words telling me that you were here for me. I should have known that the whispers in the night didn't belong only to me alone. You left me all alone living for the weekend killing me softly with her words. She told me your flavor because you didn't have the courage to tell me the truth. The dreams turned into nightmares. the laughter turned into screaming! How could you pretend to be a champion hero all along you were a thief in the night!

Never mind the lost vows broken promises from an empty heart. The entertainment was that of a clown in a three-ring circus. Strangest fragrance I ever smelled on you. Must of a loose woman who made you feel like you were invincible. Her lies tickled your eardrums. You were under a spell. This is why I filed for the divorce papers scattered all over my bedroom floor! I dressed up nice for court you see this was the best decision I ever made! Leaving you though you had never joined me. Unequally yoked no surprise why things just didn't work out. I lost a ton of weight fluid poured off my body like a rainstorm. Now I am finally happy to be free. I had to forgive you so my heart could heal. Now this heart transplant pumps new blood through my veins crazy how laughter burst through the pains. l don't hurt anymore or question why? I just inhale exhale and breathe really slow. Not knowing how things will go is a pleasurable surprise to me. Being held by a true love tight and lovely.

YA YA YA (MISSY YOU ARE A QUEEN)

Missy you are a QUEEN! You know how you painted the earth with contouring lines planting seeds fruit bearing trees! Your knowledge is true wisdom pure tear drops rivers sand dunes rocky planets out of this world! Hair like wool garments of royalty! Your KING came before you requested your arrival! Carving pictures and symbols into stones while planting your garden time of creation known. For centuries your ancestors told you stories of your origin's past, only in hope that your destiny will live and last! Heartbeats the rhythm of life eternal Glory delivered you from misery and strife. Create procreate be fruitful and multiple, two by two just you and i we are the children of parents who kept us growing together by and by giving homage to our ancestors for directing the way found not lost due to God we pray

LADY DI

STATUS QUO

When I first met him, I was in college. After a night of clubbing he introduced me to himself. I was hesitant about him signaling for me to let my window down at each red light. But suddenly I gave in to him. I thought about giving him a fake telephone number but, I gave him the real digits. He called me immediately and we talked until the birds started chirping. I am a singer and I am like his tune. I'm a midwest girl and he has southern charm. So back to the story, he took me out on the town to the best restaurants in the city. He fed my soul we exchanged juices. One night he took me to the club. I thought he was already 21 since he took me to forever 21. Shopping sprees, fine dining and dancing all night long. Nights turned into days and days turned into nights. We were committed to this love at first sight. I didn't see what was coming from around the corner. Homicide detectives couldn't have warned me. This time the need was a doctor not necessarily a lawyer. My red bottom heels were worn out these flu symptoms and headaches had me sleeping on my couch. So, I made an appointment with my physician and the lab drew blood. Not knowing Mr. Wright gave me HIV!

P.O.E.T. ANTHOLOGY VOLUME VI

LOVELY LYRICIST

Antoinette Coleman

LOVELY LYRICIST

LOVELY LYRICIST

Born Antoinette Coleman, Lovely Lyricist wrote poems as a child yet never kept them because she considered it doodling. She became serious about Poetry and Spoken Word in 2009 when she met International Poet Blaq Ice who was one of many poets that performed at her church Praise Temple of Restoration in Chicago, Il. Shortly after her encounter with Blaq Ice, he became her mentor, bringing out of her the hidden gifts which had been suppressed.

Lovely Lyricist began to get her first taste of live open mic poetry performance in the fall of 2009 at an open mic set hosted by Blaq Ice in which he later asked her to be his permanent Co-Host. Feeling inexperienced and shocked at the opportunity this would only be the beginning of her hosting experience. Lovely Lyricist felt this to be an honor to be asked so she conversed with God and was lead to accept the plight. Little did she know that her greatest challenge was yet to come! Hosting Strictly 4 The Listeners Open Mic set for 5 years and her own Quench Your mental thirst for a year! In March of 2010, Lovely Lyricist was asked to host the sold out Kings of Poetry, the largest Spoken Word Concert in the Midwest, at the DuSable Museum. Lovely Lyricist went on to host and perform in many other shows to name a few like Stand Up, Bedroom Diaries, Intimate Conversations, Verbal Stimulations, and the known Black Women's Expo in Chicago several times, as well as performing and mentoring at Richard T. Crane High School, her alma mater, Ace Tech High School and many other shows and venues.

In 2010, Lovely Lyricist joined the P.O.E.T. Organization and is now their International Chairperson. People of Extraordinary Talent is an Artist Activist Organization of everyday, hardworking, *people* who use their God given talent to reach those in need of change. Lovely Lyricist believes in the movement's mission of *"changing the world, one heart, one mind, one verse at a time."* Lovely Lyricist writes with the thought of implanting into others with hopes that they inspire someone as well. She truly believes that 'God is Love, Love is Life, Life is LOVELY and meant to be lived spreading love and living a peaceful life.'

Lovely Lyricist became a published author 12-12-12, her work can be found in Englewood Expressions as well as other volumes of P.O.E.T Anthology. She continues to host and perform at several events as well as mentors wherever needed. She has hosted and performed at numerous events in Chicago, Indiana, Detroit, Jamaica & Mexico including Stand Up in which was the debut of her 1st Spoken Word CD - RESTORED in May of 2013.

Email: lovelylyricist@comcast.net ~ Phone: 708-539-4823

LOVELY LYRICIST

Love...

The love she wants can't be in phases

Can't be set up like stanzas on big pages

Has to have a constant flow like the niagara

Needing no help from the blue pill, viagra

Love falling like the snow in the winter or rain in the spring

Not that ole fair weather love

But one of all seasons

Love for her filled with just because reasons

A love that is true and pure with no facades

Love sent and guided by God!

The Perfect Piece

I, want that yearn back
I want to be able to write that perfect piece
You know, the one that tells exactly what is going on deep inside of me
But I CAN'T……
Because every time I start to write my mind goes on a rant
My heart takes over and starts running my cup over with……
All of the hurt and pain I've experienced in the past
All of the hurt and pain that I truly thought I had got pass
Let go, set free so that I could move on and truly be me

I, want that yearn back
I want to be able to sit down and write that piece about the peace in me
Is it a problem that I just want to write that happy piece?
You know the one that will uplift the entire audience
Have em' crying happy tears while jumping out of their seats
On their feet saying things like go head girl and rewind to me
But this, this piece right here, ain't that piece
Because somewhere inside of me I seem to still be seeking peace
Something is stirring in my being that simply won't let me be!
So I just be……………………………………………………
Fake smiling and saying life is great
So I'll just hold on until my bow breaks or
Until I call out to God so hard that my spirit shakes
Either way
I'll ache through the process but………….
At some point I'll rise up
At some point my smile will be genuine and
My I'm great won't be fake
So see,

I, simply just want that yearn back
I just want to write what I feel and not simply what I lack
So I'll just keep my relationship with God
Keep sharing with the Lord the desires of my heart
Because I know that God has my back!

LOVELY LYRICIST

Truth!

Time, heals all wounds

And Love, they say is just for fools

But I say Fools tell the truth

And truth is all she wanted was- the truth

No lies just to get what he wanted

But truth that even if not on the same page

He'd be willing to let her go

Be willing to take a chance on losing her temporarily

Instead of losing her respect forever

See, all she wanted was the truth

And even though Time heals all wounds

From his lies, started the journey of her broken heart

And the love he thought was forever be the love he would lose!

We are Not just Black History we are (His) story

From the moment we proved to be the Kings and Queens God blessed us to be

People have tried to minimize our existence physically, spiritually and most of all mentally

Why, because we are not just black history, We Are (His) story!

We have been fighting for our lives since the moment we were enslaved

Truth is because the world knows the intelligence in which we've been graced

The greatness that God has placed within us all to be a success

Has caused many to come against us trying to make us feel as if we are a disgrace

We are strong, mighty and intelligent human beings

Formed by the same God that formed every other man, woman, boy and girl

Yet we have been treated as if we are not of this world

Why because we are not just black history we are (His) story!

We are Not just Black History we are (His) story (2)

We have proven throughout our lives that no matter the plight before us

We are a blessed people and many just simply don't want to compete with us

Why else would they steal our inventions and try to say they are their own

Break up our families yet have us enslaved to build up their homes

They know the truth that there's greatness within us

So today I need you to know what they know to help build us back up

Let's unite to show those before us that their fights were not in vain

By continuing (His) Story and becoming positive and life changing History

We are Not just Black History we are (His) story (3)

Because of blacks the world has thrived in many ways:

Did you know Thomas Jennings stands in history as the first black person to receive a patent? Although he was well known as a tailor Jennings was unhappy that his customer's clothes were becoming soiled and could not be cleaned in the normal fashion so he sought out to find a process to help them. That process in 1820 was called dry scouring today we know it as dry cleaning.

Did you know Thomas Elkins in 1879 designed a device that helped with the task of preserving perishable foods by way of refrigeration? He also had previously patented a chamber commode in 1872 and an ironing table w/ quilt frame combined in 1870.

We are Not just Black History we are (His) story (4)

And did you know, Madame C.J. Walker was having problems with losing her hair and tried all she could by using products to help her hair but to no avail. According to history Madam Walker had a dream in which a black man appeared to her and told her what to mix up for her hair.

Although some of the remedy was grown in Africa she sent for it, put it on her scalp, and her hair started growing back within weeks. She then tested this product on friends with great success she started selling the product.

Realizing that blacks had very few options for hair care products she along with her new husband started the Madam CJ Walker Manufacturing Company, bringing in her daughter later to manage the company, Madam Walker travelled the country marketing her products bringing on other women to help her with sales and marketing, this allowed her to become known as the first black woman millionaire in 1914 after 9 years of working hard at something she believed in.

This is proof that in time with hard work anything can be achieved.

We are Not just Black History we are (His) story (5)

I could keep going because there are many more who we may not have been made aware of

Many who took the gifts given by God to show the world what we are made of!

And although today we are still fighting what seems to be a never-ending battle

We can continue to change the world and what they want to think of us by continuing to be more than just black history but by showing the world that we are and forever will be a major part of (His) Story

So today I challenge you to make dreams come true like Dr. King

Research our history and share it 365 days of the year

Let the world know that we are NOT just about history one month out of the year but we are historical every day because we are a major part of (His) Story.

Why I Love to Hate what God Created (Nature)

Ground thawing out now first buds of green
Clothes wet and now I'm cold, how I hate to be cold
Worms and other creatures can't wait to be seen
Scene is Spring
Although I love the new green leaves I hate the rain
I know, I know we need it for the world to grow, like grain
So I tolerate it because it makes the beauty glow
Love it because it makes the rivers flow
Reasons why I Love to Hate What God Created

So hot I'm sweating like I'm running a race
Beautiful trees but their seeds are all over the ground
I have a strange phobia of stepping on them now,
And then I would go for a swim but I am afraid
The beach is beautiful as the waves hit the sand
And I wonder how something so marvelous
Can be so helpful and dangerous
Birds flying over us dropping their nasty dew
Yet the robin is so beautiful as it sings for you
Many are gathered in Holy matrimony
As the birds are demanding to be seen
The scene is summer
Reasons why I Love to Hate What God Created

Different hues of beautiful leaves fall to the ground
Almost profound that this stage is almost like death
Rain flowing more although those things that should grow
Are about to hibernate like the forest bear
Not to be seen out without a sweater or light jacket
Cause you might get cold or caught in the rain
Such a beautiful time of the year as it starts to unfold
Hold on to your umbrella, pocket book and coat
As the wind blows again because it's cold
Starts looking spooky outside
Since the leaves are dying and the flowers
Look like they have no life

Now all that seems to want to be seen is not life
Scene is fall
Reasons why I Love to hate What God Created

As beautiful as it seems the snow is so overrated
Falling down from heaven covering the world like a blanket
Yet blankets are meant to keep you warm
Snow and ice freezes all life forms
The birds migrate and the bears hibernate
My question is then why do I have to stay
Covered with large coats, gloves, scarves and boots
People playing making snow balls with plans of hitting you
Best thing about the season is that Christmas comes
A time of the year where love is spread with plenty of cheer
Only a few animals like the snow like the reindeer
The dirt is so hard nothing can survive there
Can't wait for the thaw again so I can again see green
So I can marvel at the beautiful flowers and hear the birds
But wait as I wake the scene is still winter
So I keep the beautiful aspects of it in my head
Because if not my creativity becomes dead
Reasons why I Love to Hate what God Created

Yet I Love life and all Life forms because God created them!

P.O.E.T. ANTHOLOGY VOLUME VI

Belief is the fundamental building blocks of possibilities.

DR. H

hülya n. yılmaz

HULYA N. YILMAZ ... DR. H

Liberal Arts Emerita, hülya n. yılmaz is a published author, literary translator, and Co-Chair and Director of Editing Services at Inner Child Press International. Her poetic work appeared in an excess of eighty-five anthologies of global endeavors and has been presented at numerous national and international poetry events. In 2018, the Writer's International Network of British Colombia, Canada honored yılmaz with a literary award. As of 2017, two of her poems remain permanently installed in *Telepoem Booth* – a U.S.-wide poetic art exhibition. hülya finds it vital for everyone to understand a deeper sense of self, and writes creatively to attain a comprehensive awareness for and development of our humanity.

A New Day Dawned . . . Again

Sipping coffee in the comfort of a home
Running water, heat, food and peace intact
Luxuries for too many on Earth
Their sufferings . . . oh, do they impact!
Knots in the throat, tears in the heart
While sitting on the privileged throne
Knowing that there is so much to unearth
And needing to reach out with a helping hand

Oh, the soul pains severely
Over the aches of the known
And the still-unknown

Yet she goes on to stay inside her frame
And devours by now-cold coffee,
One sip at a time . . .

and . . .

the slumber sleeps on

what are facts but an illusion
when wrapped in orchestrated lies
when displayed on trays of make-believe
that the sleepers rush to devour
behind their tightly closed blinds

as for their hearts . . .

the slumber sleeps on

cries

i hear cries
the cries of children
i cannot see them but i know
those hefty tears are there to stay
frozen in mid-air, frozen in helplessness
in hopelessness and in utter fiery despair
for we, grown-ups have chosen to be quiet
yet once again, numb, deaf and delusional
so delusional that we wake up every single day
to the comfort and convenience of our petty lives
lives so petty that we insist to insist on and on
not to care, not to think, not to sense, not to feel
all along dismissing what stirs up deep inside
our consciousness, our gut instincts, our compassion
our original purpose: to love, to love them all

"why?" asks one of those icons of innocence
"what have I done to deserve this fate?"
not in words, as not all know how to speak yet
their eyes say it all, eyes filled with salty drops
instead of tummy-giggles,
instead of daily, nightly jumps of joy,
instead of cushioned care-free slumbers,
instead of the tender safety of love's embrace

"why?"
why are there so many cries?

Early Morning . . .

The silence of the new day called my name.
To hear it is a fierce struggle.
Indoors and outdoors,
the so-called modern world
is up already.

Shame is on me.
What a shame!

Hearing the noise of my mind anew,
while nature spreads its grace before me
on a table of gently rustling tree branches,
scurrying little critters - no birds in sight yet.
I miss them so!

I wanted to listen to my breath.
I craved to hear my heartbeat,
like that of a newborn
to cleanse my soul from all the ills
humanity has crafted for itself for too long.

Oh, I do long,
long for the calm, the quiet
so much so that I feel much unease
at the sound of my thoughts, my worries.

I wanted to listen to my breath.
I craved to hear my heartbeat,
like that of a newborn
to cleanse my soul from all the ills
humanity has crafted for itself for too long.

my friend, the wind

take away the tears
take away the worries
they are Man-crafted, can you not see?
playgrounds were once meant for giggles
where have all the tummy-laughs gone?
what are we doing? what have we done?
broken promises, lost souls galore
tender hearts, unable to smile anymore

my friend, the wind sat down with me again
attempting to cleanse off of my core the pain
there used to be a time when a gentle breeze
felt aplenty to keep my aching mind at ease
the more i age the more i sink into a sorrow,
for hope is being rubbed from babies' 'morrow

take away the tears
take away the worries
they are Man-crafted, can you not see?

JUST BILL

William S. Peters, Sr.

WILLIAM S. PETERS, SR.

WILLIAM S. PETERS, SR.

AKA 'just bill', William S. Peters, Sr. is a devoted writer who has been committed to the path of poetry since 1966. Presently, his poetic work has been published in excess of 200 anthologies, newspapers and literary magazines, including in excess 50 books of his own. Since the day of his commitment to the creation and public-sharing of the poetic art, Peters has been a devoted supporter of the venue of creative expression –regardless of form. His conviction that the human countenance through written art is a necessity reflects in his capacity as an activist for the progression and evolution of humanity and its love of each other.

Inner Child Press International – Peters' publishing enterprise has brought attention worldwide to several hundred poets by means of the authors' personal releases and the appearances of their work in a large number of anthologies. Such undertakings encompass notable and highly acclaimed anthology series, such as the voluminous *World Healing, World Peace* –published every two years since 2012 and *The Year of the Poet* – a monthly international book as conceived in January 2014 and published every month since. In the latter anthology, The Poetry Posse –a core group of contributing poets comprises fourteen poets from a large variety of world regions. This publication also features between two and four guest poets each month.

William S. Peters, Sr., a 2016 Pulitzer Prize nominee for poetry has enjoyed the honor of being recognized for his work at large – publishing and writing alike also in the U.S., his country of birth The number of his appearances on North American radio and television shows is too copious to list. His poetic work has been published in various countries of the world, including Kosovo, Albania, Germany, Iran, Iraq, India, The Philippines, Taiwan, Canada, Italy, Romania, Saudi Arabia, Jordan, Morocco, Italy, England, Romania, France, Germany and Poland. The author is known to be adamant about taking time out to share his humanitarian, spiritual and philosophical insights wherever he is invited. He has cited and performed his poetry at numerous venues, such as summer camps for children, teacher workshops, poetry workshops and classrooms, including an October 2017-lecture to graduate students at The University of Jordan in Amman, Jordan.

The author currently serves as the CEO of Inner Child Enterprises, ltd., Managing Director of Inner Child Press International, Executive Producer of Inner Child Radio and Executive Editor of Inner Child Magazine.

For more of William S. Peters, Sr., visit his personal web site at: www.iamjustbill.com

I dream of that place

I dream of that place
I once called home,
And there is an acute longing
That pains my heart
When I remember

I have a distant hope
To once again
Feel the soles of my feet
Touch the raw damp earth
In the quiet gardens
Where solace grows
And peace is the yield
That is borne
Upon every bud and blossom

The trees of this land
Offer a sweet fruit
Of content and smiles
And we, all the children
Were kissed
By gentle breezes and sunshine

Oh, it did rain . . .
Every now and then,
and we all were cleansed
Of our errant thoughts
And our 3rd eye opened
As our brows of sweat . . .
Renewed

There were no lamentations

Yes, I dream,
I dream of that place,
That elusive place

That dances about me
Enticing me and my aspirations
For you,
For the world
For the all of all things

1 eye blind

A deep rose colored monocle
Adorns the left,
The right?

Night endures
Sight obscures
There are no sure- ities
That appease our wonder
Our quest
For truth

The test we face
Has a space ... somewhere
Out there in the nefarious ether,
The never ever neither either
Where you nor I
Can seem to get to

The anguish
Of no light,
Only blight seen
Demeans our essence,
But our very presence
Confirms the present,
Yet to come,
And validates our delusion
Pertaining the illusion s
Of the past
And the future
We must face ...
Can you taste
Your sense of it all

Worry not
About the fall,
For it has already happened
And perhaps ...

Poke me in my 3rd eye,
And perchance
I will know you are here We are flapping
Broken wings
Attempting to fly
In the liquid soup
Of subterfugeous dis-chord

1 eye blind,
The other adorns
A deeply colored
Rose flavored monocle

Smell the flowers my child
Smell the flowers,
For therein lies
The hope you have yet
To grasp.

With me

So I did

She sharpened the pencil . . . deliberately
Then raised it on high
Above her spiritual aura
And then stabbed me . . .
Again deliberately
In my heart

She began to etch
Words and verse,
Lyrics dispersed
Upon the walls
Of my cluttered chambers of love . . .
In a 'Free-Style" sort of way,
For that is how her spirit was . . . FREE

We had no use for the eraser
During this life defying,
Edifying moment,
So, we took it, together
Between our fingers
And began to eliminate, erase
All the dimly lit vibrations about us
That expectorated anything less
Than brilliance

And then the music played,
Once again
As it had done
O so long ago
In the days of my youth

I thanked her
For the gift,
This perceivable world,
Where I let and bled
All the poisons

I have ingested
And collected
Along my selected, defected . . . way

I smiled as I reflected
And inspected
The 'who am I',
And I remembered succinctly
That I loved to dance . . .
So I did

Out there huh?

Push button memories
And
Instant daisies
Growing out of that pot I sketched
In my note book
While sitting on
My Blue Roof
In my Blue Moment

Kent Newburn says to me
That these times
Are keepers,
Jeepers mom,
Can you play that back
Again?

Kent Newburn says to me
That these times
Are keepers

We too often forget
What is important ...
Is it the memories
We create and construct
In our dimly lit halls
Of cognizance?
Or the flowers we produce
Along the way ...
Chances are,
It's a hodge podge

Say,
What was Alice's boyfriend's name,
Did he go to Wonderland as well,
If so, I betcha by golly wow,
She will never tell ...

In the meantime
All the Kings and Princes
And a few Princesses too,
The Governors and Rulers,
And Oligarchs few
Sang in concert
The Lechers Anthem
While on the hunt
For innocence
To be defiled ...
Keep a very close eye
On your child and children,
For they are not safe
In this world
That has been heralded ...
In and out
The revolving door goes
While we are far too busy
Sticking our noses
Where it does not belong,
Like up the wrong asses

The other day
While sitting in class
At Film School
I wrote a script,
Kind of silly of sort
About how we can abort
All of the nonsense
Before we all
Are poisoned ....

I really did not want to share
Such an ominous thing,
So I wrote this poem instead
About all the crazy stuff
Floating around
In my head ...

WILLIAM S. PETERS, SR.

The only thing is,
I can not remember
Whether or not
This is a push button memory
Or something I sketched
Called 'Instant Daisies' ...
Out there huh?

The Saviour is late

Somewhere in the vast darkness
Where light should have been,
The silence was blossoming
As 'Reason' began
To spread its crippled wings

The ignorance was infectious
And a once sacred balance
We species possessed
Had lost it's way

The innate hunger
Of those thirsty for expansion,
For growth,
For clarity,
Now lay upon the roadside
As the blind ones,
The univested wayfarers of life
Numbly,
Rotefully,
Whispered incantations
Unto their own hearts,
Their children,
Seeking to deliberately
Maintain the inauthentic veil
That allowed their
Sleep
To go undisturbed

This is what we have come to,
A quintessential quest-less existence
Where truth had become
A discordant raspy sound,
An annoyance
That aided and abetted
Our dis-ease

WILLIAM S. PETERS, SR.

Fortunately,
Somewhere in the realm
Of the obscure dreams
Of a few,
There was a light
That was beginning to
Consume their souls
Seeking to purge the despair
And melancholy
That loomed about,
Promising to vanquish the illusion
Of an impending doom ...

But it shall not be,
Nay, it shall not
For the darkness
Can not prophesize
It's own demise
With any certainty,
Without the light

The Saviour is late,
And our fate unfortunately
Is in our own hands.

EPILOGUE

may the Grace of God be sufficient . . .

P.O.E.T.

Fallen Soldiers

Strawberri Taylor

9 October 1965 ~ 19 March 2019

P.O.E.T. PICTURES

Strawberri Taylor was a Spoken Word Mogul who changed the game of Spoken Word stage shows in America. Although she was an American poet, her reach spanned across the world. She was known as The Queen Of Erotic Poetry. Her stage shows garnered $75 per ticket and upward. This was done with the backing of cooperate sponsorship. She had a traveling stage show called Verbal Intercourse which shocked onlookers and gave thousands of fans something to talk about months after leaving her productions. She brought exotic dancers, erotic poets, stage skits and vocalist all together to create the perfect erotic experience. Her shows may have started in Chicago but Vegas eventually caught wind and she expanded to the Vegas strip.

In addition to her stage persona and erotic stage shows, she did her share of community work, helping to transform lives in her community. She was part of the leadership and the advisory board President with the international P.O.E.T organization and the one who was responsible for introducing P.O.E.T President, king of poetry Blaq Ice to Spoken Word in the Fall of 2000. Strawberri achieved so much during her reign as Queen of erotic Poetry, but never forgot about those whose paths she crossed on her way to the top. Strawberri gave opportunities to several poets in the poetry community and helped to launch many careers in Spoken Word.

In March of 2019 Strawberri lost her decades long battle with cancer and passed away peaceably in her daughter's home surrounded by family and close friends. She will forever be missed, but never will she be forgotten. Her shows may have stopped, but her legacy will live on forever. Long live Strawberri Taylor, The Queen Of Erotic Poetry.

P.O.E.T. ANTHOLOGY VOLUME VI

Remembering Mz Conception
Consuela Jones

21 September 1974 ~ 15 October 2016

P.O.E.T® PICTURES

Janet Perkins Caldwell

14 February 1957 ~ 20 September 2016

P.O.E.T. ANTHOLOGY VOLUME VI

Terri Nsypre Lee

15 November 1953 ~ 3 February 2017

P.O.E.T® PICTURES

Angela "whatshaname" Hoskins

11 October 1968 ~ 28 March 2015

P.O.E.T. ANTHOLOGY VOLUME VI

High Yellow Prince

23 December 1961 ~ 23 September 2015

P.O.E.T.® Pictures

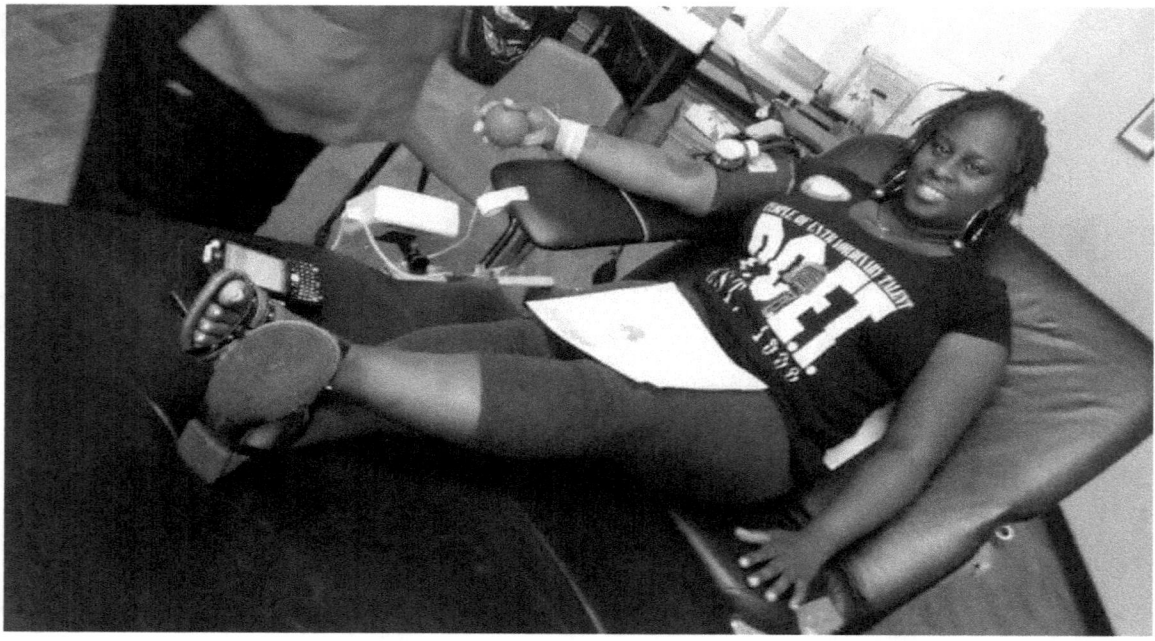

Not only does the P.O.E.T® movement donate their talent and time to the community, they also donate blood in annual Chicago blood drives.

P.O.E.T. PICTURES

P.O.E.T® on the move, turning our words into A.C.T.I.O.N.

Every year the P.O.E.T. movement performs on the R.A.G.E. (Resident Association for Greater Englewood) tour in Chicago's Englewood Neighboorhood. On this one stage was P.O.E.T. members from Kansas, Washington D.C., New York, California, Wisconsin and Chicago.

The P.O.E.T. movement helped to sponsor a back to the books school supply drive in Flint Michigan led by P.O.E.T. all-star Donnis Overton aka Black Beauty. Hundreds of school supplies were given away to the children of Flint.

P.O.E.T® PICTURES

P.O.E.T® on the move, turning our words into A.C.T.I.O.N.

Every year P.O.E.T does a homeless coat drive to help those who are need during the winter season.

P.O.E.T. on the move, turning our words into A.C.T.I.O.N. !!!

Every Thanksgiving the P.O.E.T. organization volunteers to feed the community as a part of our community outreach program

P.O.E.T. PICTURES

P.O.E.T. on the move, turning our words into action !!!

Every year the P.O.E.T. movement through our Tyrone Hawthorne cancer / scholarship foundation donates $1,000.00 to a graduating senior to assist them with their books and travel expenses.

P.O.E.T® on the move, turning our words into action !!!

The P.O.E.T® movement throws annual stay in school / save our children rallies, encouraging and instilling in our youth that they are God's gift to the world.

P.O.E.T. on the move, turning our words into action !!!

P.O.E.T. speaks with FWLOI

Families With Loved Ones Incarcerated

P.O.E.T® on the move, turning our words into action !!!

P.O.E.T®'s March for Non Violence

P.O.E.T. PICTURES

P.O.E.T®'s International President Blaq Ice with President Barack Obama

P.O.E.T. ANTHOLOGY VOLUME VI

P.O.E.T. with R&B legend Tony Terry

P.O.E.T® PICTURES

P.O.E.T® receives an honor at Teen Summit

P.O.E.T. ANTHOLOGY VOLUME VI

P.O.E.T. Presents
The Tyrone Hawthorne Scholarship

P. O. E.T® Mentors at the Kroc Center in Chicago

P. O. E.T® Merchandise

P.O.E.T. PICTURES

P. O. E.T.
with the Legendary King of House Music Farley Jackmaster Funk

P.O.E.T. ANTHOLOGY VOLUME VI

P. O. E.T. Presents The Tyrone Hawthorne Scholarship

P.O.E.T. PICTURES

P.O.E.T. with Lorenz Tate

P.O.E.T. ANTHOLOGY VOLUME VI

P.O.E.T.

Links and Contact Information

WEB SITE

www.iampoet.org

TELEPHONE

Toy Ann McCray
Vice President
(708) 267-9725

P.O.E.T. Radio

www.TalkShoe.com/TC/93155

724.444.7444

Access
93155#

P.O.E.T. on FaceBook

http://www.facebook.com/groups/131331986916375/

It's a blessing to be one.

~Black Beauty

P.O.E.T.
Other Anthologies

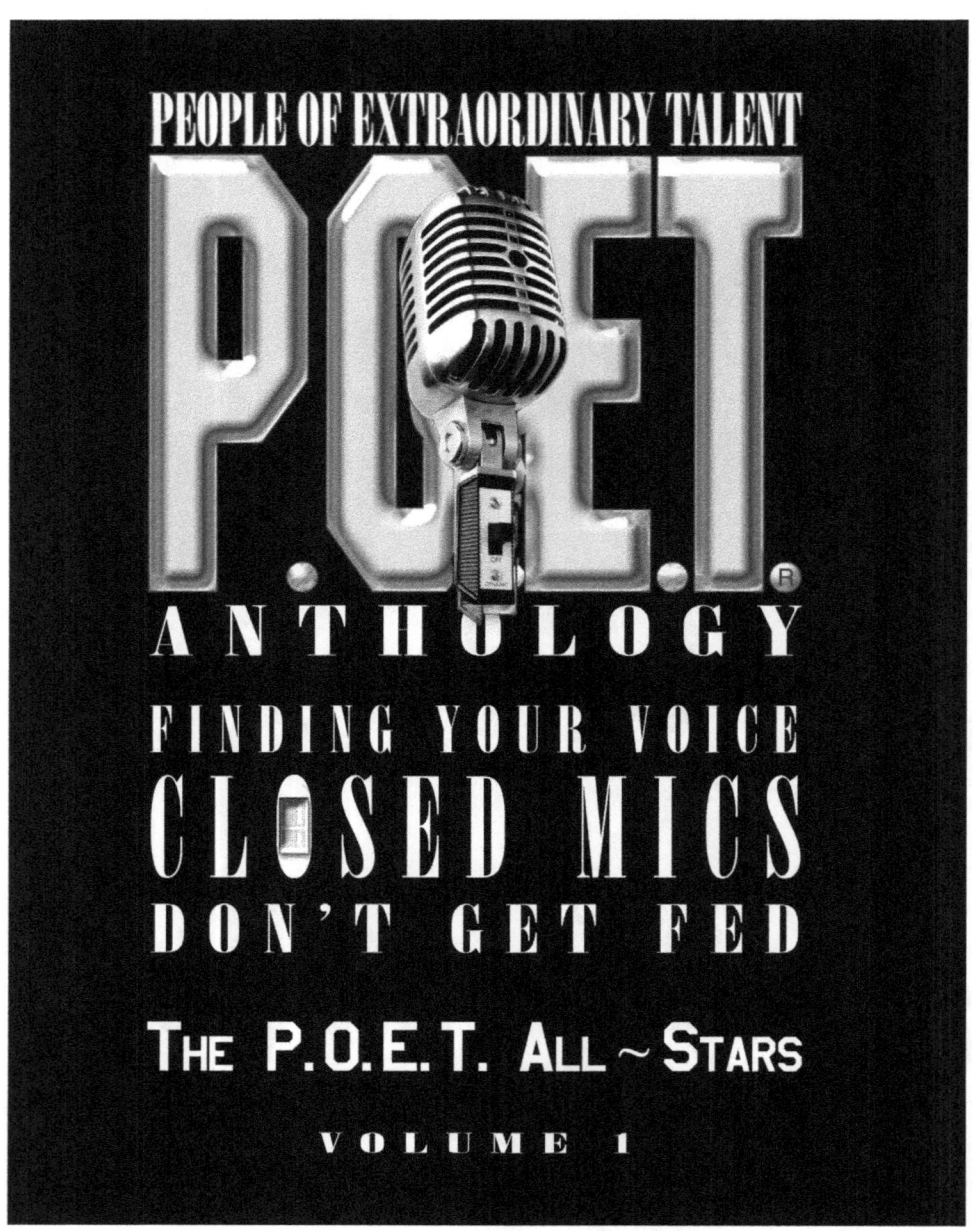

P.O.E.T. ANTHOLOGY VOLUME I
http://www.innerchildpress.com/poet-organization.php

P.O.E.T. ANTHOLOGY VOLUME II
http://www.innerchildpress.com/poet-organization.php

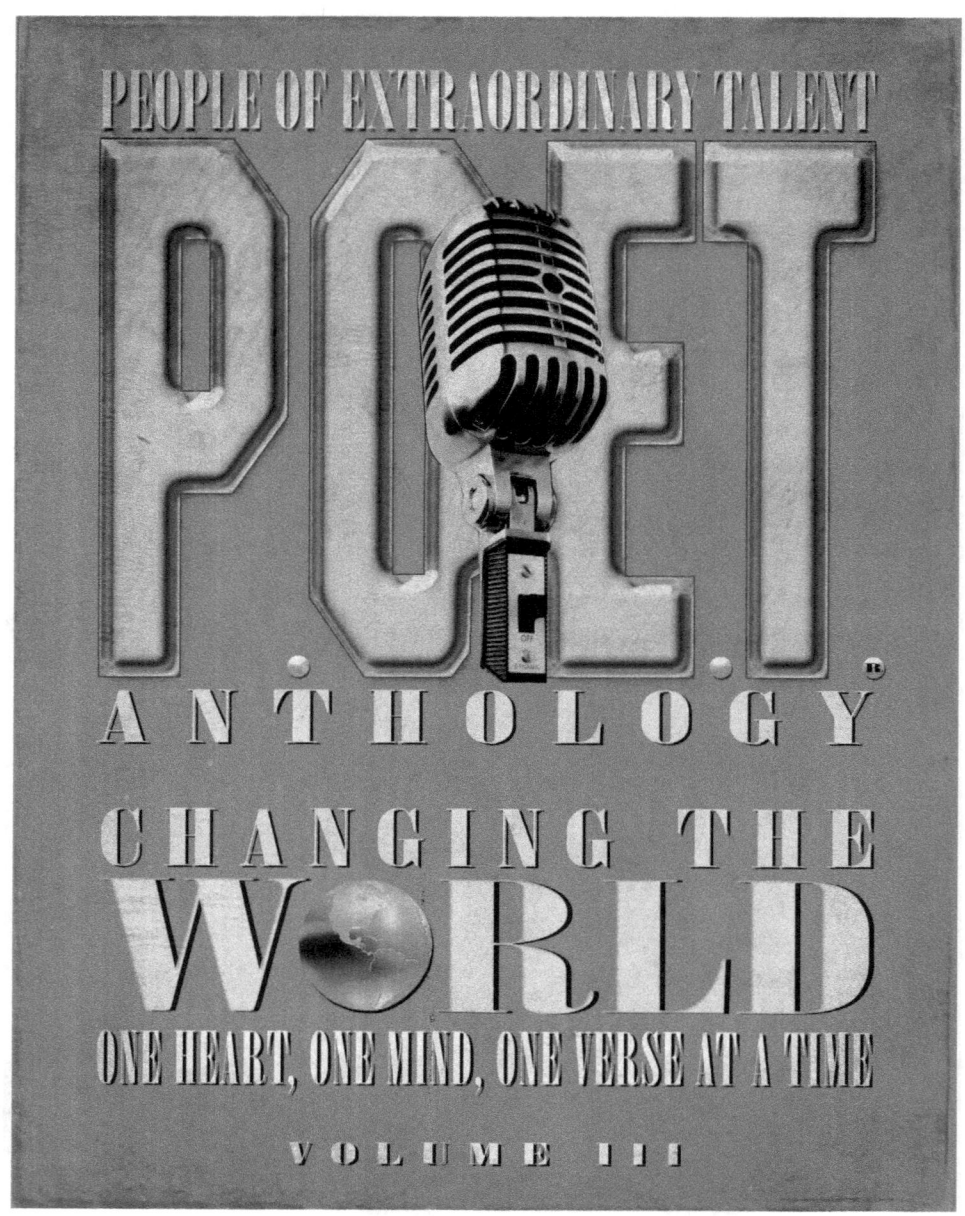

P.O.E.T. ANTHOLOGY VOLUME III
http://www.innerchildpress.com/poet-organization.php

P.O.E.T. ANTHOLOGY VOLUME IV

http://www.innerchildpress.com/poet-organization.php

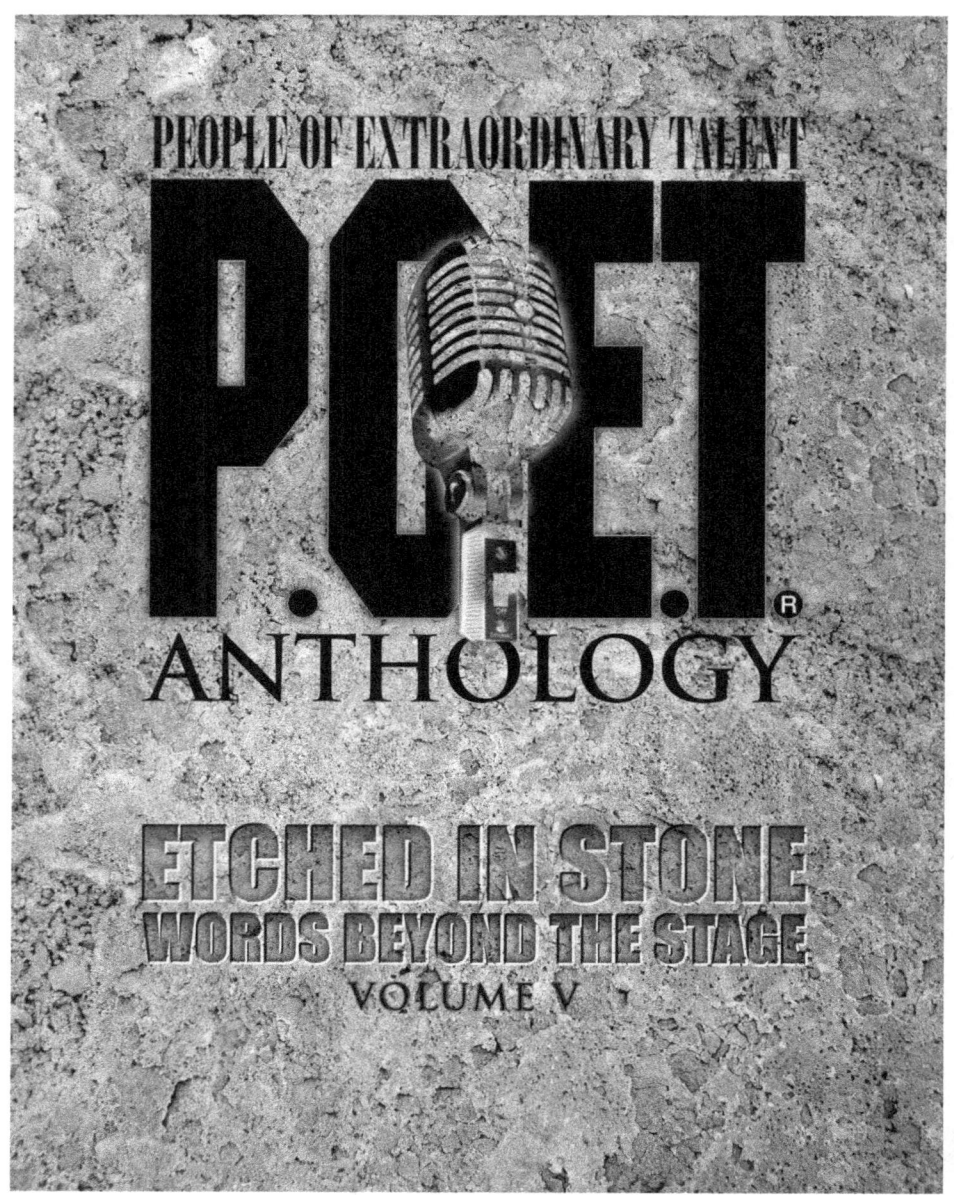

P.O.E.T. ANTHOLOGY VOLUME V

http://www.innerchildpress.com/poet-organization.php

Let your voice be heard, for God hears all things . . .
The cries, the whispers and the prayers.

P.O.E.T. ANTHOLOGY VOLUME VI

Inner Child Press

Inner Child Press is a Publishing Company Founded and Operated by Writers. Our personal publishing experiences provides us an intimate understanding of the sometimes daunting challenges Writers, New and Seasoned may face in the Business of Publishing and Marketing their Creative "Written Work".

For more Information

Inner Child Press

www.innerchildpress.com

intouch@innerchildpress.com

'building bridges of cultural understanding'

www.innerchildpress.com

www.ingramcontent.com/pod-product-compliance
Lightning Source LLC
Chambersburg PA
CBHW081835170426
43199CB00017B/2736